Winning Methods
of Bluffing & Betting *in*
POKER

Lynne Taetzsch

Sterling Publishing Co., Inc.
New York

For my father, William K. Taetszch,
who first taught me to love the game.

Library of Congress Cataloging-in-Publication Data Available

10 9 8 7 6 5 4 3 2 1

Published by Sterling Publishing Co., Inc.
387 Park Avenue South, New York, NY 10016
© 1976, 2002 by Lynne Taetzsch
Distributed in Canada by Sterling Publishing
c/o Canadian Manda Group, One Atlantic Avenue, Suite 105
Toronto, Ontario, Canada M6K 3E7
Distributed in Great Britain by Chrysalis Books
64 Brewery Road, London N7 9NT, England
Distributed in Australia by Capricorn Link (Australia) Pty. Ltd.
P.O. Box 704, Windsor, NSW 2756, Australia

Manufactured in the United States of America

ISBN: 1-4027-1628-1

Contents

 # **Introduction**

As a poker fan and regular player, I've been an avid reader of the poker books on the market. Many of them have been very useful. It does help to know what the chances are of a particular hand winning a game, how the number of players changes the odds, the chances of drawing a particular card, and so forth.

I played for years in a weekly game in a university town. Most players were professors, or in some way connected to the college. They played an intellectual game in which the important thing was to play smart. Winnings were merely an indicator of one's cleverness.

One of the players—let's call him Dave—really had an ego investment in the game. He had read all the poker books and prided himself on his effective strategy. He wanted so badly for us all to know how smart he was that he was constantly giving other players advice, or pointing out their stupid errors. When I first entered the game, I thought Dave was the best player there.

But then I noticed that the big winner in the game was a guy who never talked about his skill. While Dave drank coffee and concentrated, Tom drank beer and appeared to be having a good time. He seemed to be a rather inconsistent player, actually, and I wondered what made him win so much.

After lengthy observation, I realized that, while Dave made careful decisions based on probabilities, concentrating mainly on *his own hand*, Tom played more by *reacting to the other players*. He was a good reader—of cards and people. He was also a good bluffer. It was extremely difficult to predict what *he* might do at any given time. And thirdly, he knew how to bet in order to gain the maximum value from a particular hand.

In order to do well at any competitive game, you've got to know your competition and what makes them tick. In tennis, for example, if you know your opponent has a weak backhand, that's where you'll try to place the ball. In addition, if you can intimidate your opponent by acting aggressive, this is a good psychological tactic to use. Even in sports, physical skill is not the only criterion for winning. In poker, much more than card skills are required to be a consistent big winner. For after you've figured out all the possibilities and probabilities, you're still faced with the question: "Did the guy catch or is he bluffing?" Even a one-in-fifty chance will happen one in fifty times. Is this the time?

Poker is not like other card games. I've watched many a tournament bridge player enter our poker game and go away red-faced and broke. That's because brainpower, strategies, and card-sense do not begin to cover what poker's all about. There's no best way to play a particular poker hand. It's like the game of life: The more you're aware of the total situation and the more you control the action, the more power and effectiveness you have.

How are you at bluffing in your life? Can you walk into the boss's office and demand a raise? Or if you're the boss, how do you handle employees who threaten to strike unless they get their demands? Do you know when they mean it and when they're bluffing? Can you put up a counter-bluff?

One experience with the bluff we have all had is driving a car. When other drivers try to pull in front of you into your lane, do you let them? More important, are you aware which drivers know what they're doing and which are oblivious to your car? That's important to know. If you try a counter-bluff on an incompetent driver who's not aware of your presence, it could mean an accident. The same thing in poker. There's no point in trying to bluff a poor player who is unaware of what you're doing. Your bluff will be wasted.

So awareness of what's happening around you is crucial to winning poker. When you know what's going on in the other guy's head—why he's raising $10 or why he's drawing two cards or why he's replacing his 9♠—then you can decide what is the best action for you to take. And just as it's important for you to be able to read the other players, it's important that you don't let them read you. Be a master of the bluff, and you'll win at poker.   —Lynne Taetzsch

Reading Cards

THE IMPORTANT THING IN POKER is not how many winning hands you're dealt, but being able to distinguish them from the losing hands. This means you must be able to read your opponents' cards and interpret their play. If you know the relative strength and possibilities of all the hands on the table, you'll know whether to drop, call, bet, or raise.

There are a number of poker books on the market that will tell you the required strength you must have in your own hand to stay in the game. For example, in seven-card stud you're normally told to have a pair of jacks or better in the first three cards, in order to see the next card. These rules are fine for the beginning poker player, and will at least protect you from some losses.

But unless you play with some bunch of dodos, you have to look past your own hand. The real skill and money-making talent in poker is to be able to read your opponents, and then use that information successfully by placing the proper bets. These are the poker skills that will put big bills in your pocket at the end of an evening.

Basic Reading Skills

The first place to look for information from your opponents' hands is in the cards themselves. Carefully analyze all cards on the table. For example, in a seven-card stud if you see a player with four hearts showing, you know there's a good chance he's got a flush. You might see two or three possibilities in a hand. The important thing is to be aware of them.

Now, when you're looking at possibilities, don't just concentrate on what a player's got in his own hand. You've got to consider *all* the cards known to you. For example, if a guy's got two aces, you figure he could have three or four aces. Yeah, he *could*, except that there's another ace showing in another hand, and one folded the previous round. This illustration brings home the point that you've got to remember the cards that are folded. One of those forgotten cards may mean the difference between winning and losing the pot.

In most circles, it's up to the individual to remember what cards are on the table, so that when somebody folds, it's up to you to have seen and remembered what he's got. If you ask, "What did you fold?" you'll get silence or the wrong answer. This is why you've got to be constantly alert as to what's happening around you, not lost in your own hand's possibilities. Encourage the players in your group to fold in turn only, in order to make it easier to see and remember what's being folded.

In our Thursday night group, Steve was always trying to make rules to regulate the game. He wanted to make a rule whereby everybody had to say what their up cards were out loud when they folded. The rest of us wouldn't agree to this. But whenever a new player came in the game, he'd tell them he'd appreciate it if they'd call out their cards before they folded. To promote this behavior, he thanked them profusely whenever they remembered to do it. If someone folded without telling him what their cards were, he'd often ask what they were, and most players would tell him.

Finally, we got a new player one night who refused to cooperate with Steve. Everyone backed up the new player, and Steve was finally silenced. Generally, most groups feel it's the players responsibility to look at the cards on the board and remember them before they're folded.

That brings us to a general problem area in poker—there are no set rules of play as there are in other card games such as bridge. While you may find rules in one poker book, you can find different rules in another. This being so, most groups play house rules or develop their own rules by voting on issues as they come up. Because differences occur about these issues, the psychologically skillful player can utilize these disagreements to his own advantage. We'll discuss this later on.

Getting back to basic reading skills—let's look at a few sample hands and see what information we can get out of them:

Player:	1	2	3	4	5	6
Card 1						
Card 2						
Card 3	J♥	8♠	5♠	K♥	8♦	K♦
Card 4	9♥	Q♠	4♥	3♦	10♦	3♠
Card 5	8♣	5♥	6♣	A♠	9♣	3♥
Card 6	Q♦	K♠	10♠	6♦	10♥	2♦
Card 7						

Looking at the up cards in these six hands, what are the possibilities? In hand #1 we see a possible straight (8, 9, , J, Q). There are no pairs and only two hearts toward a flush. Looking around, we note that three 10s are showing in other hands. This means there is only one 10 out to fill in the straight in hand #1. There are six hearts showing in other hands, plus the two in hand #1, meaning there are five hearts out; #1 must have three of these in order to make a flush.

Hand #2 shows three spades for a flush. There are only three spades showing in other hands, meaning there are seven available and #2 needs only two of those. The queen and king in hand #2 make two cards toward a straight, which means the other three would have to fill in with 10, jack, ace, or 9, 10, jack. There are two 9s out, three 10s out, one jack out, and one ace out.

Hand #3's best possibility is a straight, with 4, 5, and 6 showing. However, there are three 3s and three 8s showing in other hands. Hand #3 has two spades toward a flush.

Hand #4 shows two hearts and two diamonds toward a flush, or two cards to a straight. There are six hearts and five diamonds showing in other hands.

Hand #5 shows three cards to a straight (8, 9, 10) and a pair of 10s. There's one 10 on the board, indicating the impossibility of four 10s but the possibility of three 10s or a full house. For the straight, there are no 7s and only one jack showing in other hands.

Hand #6 has a pair of 3s, a 2–3 for a straight, and two diamonds for a flush. There's another 3 showing, leaving open the possibility of two pair, three 3s, or a full house. There are five other diamonds out.

Now let's turn up the down cards and see what hands these players actually ended up with:

Player:	1	2	3	4	5	6
Card 1	9 ◇	J ◇	5 ♣	2 ♣	7 ◇	4 ♠
Card 2	Q ♡	Q ♣	2 ♠	3 ♣	6 ♠	J ♣
Card 3	J ◇	8 ♠	5 ♠	K ♡	8 ◇	K ◇
Card 4	9 ♡	Q ◇	4 ♡	3 ◇	10 ◇	3 ♠
Card 5	8 ♣	5 ♡	6 ♣	A	9 ♣	3 ♡
Card 6	Q ◇	K ♠	10 ♠	6 ◇	10 ♡	2 ◇
Card 7	9 ♠	2 ♡	6 ♡	7 ♠	8 ♡	K ♣

Player #1 had the big catch in this game. With a 9 and queen for hole cards, a 9 and queen showing, he was dealt a 9 on the last card, giving him a winning, hidden hand. The other players would probably figure he caught his straight, or possibly a flush if he bet heavily. However, his great hand is wasted this time because no one else can even beat the straight he might have caught. The next best hand is player #5, who caught his straight (a possibility we predicted).

Player #2 didn't get his spade flush, and ended up with a pair of queens. Player #3 didn't get his straight, but caught another 5 and a 6 to make two pair. Player #4 had nothing much showing, and ended up with a pair of 3s. Player #6 turned his pair of 3s into two pair.

From this example you can see that good, solid card reading skills are important. Even though they don't give you *all* the information you need to win, they do provide the groundwork. Check your reading skills out at the next poker game. Make prediction about the other players' hands, based on the cards you see, and then match predictions with reality at the end of the game.

We've been talking about stud poker so far. In draw, of course, there are no open cards to look at. But you do get some information—the number of cards that are drawn. The player who draws three cards is probably drawing to a pair; two cards means he has three of a kind (some players will draw two cards to a flush or a straight); and one card means he's looking for a flush or a straight, or has two pair.

In hi-low games, a draw of one card *usually* means the player is going low, although he could have two pair, or four to a flush or straight. Be sure to remember how many cards each player draws, and then match your predictions at the end of the game. Some players will consistently draw the same amount of cards for specific hands. Others will vary it, trying to throw you off. For example, a player with one pair may draw two cards instead of three to make you think he's got three of a kind. Some players will stay pat and bluff.

Combine Betting Observations With Card Reading

It isn't enough to simply observe a player's possibilities based on the cards he's showing. You must be aware also of the changes in his betting as he gets each new card. For example, if a player shows two hearts in his open cards, and suddenly starts raising when he's dealt another heart, you can guess that he's either caught his flush already or is mighty sure of getting it.

A player who starts out betting heavily, but slows down and merely calls, is probably not getting the cards he needed to fill in his original good possibility. Some players who are dealt good cards initially will stay in until the end, no matter what. We had such a player in our group. Joey got so excited and sure of himself when he was dealt two or three good cards, that he stayed in even though the odds mounted against him by the fourth, fifth, and sixth cards. He felt, somehow, that a guy who was dealt a pair of aces in the hole has *got* to win—*deserves* to win—in spite of the four bum cards that came next and the possible flushes and straights staring at him from other players' hands.

Normally a player will bet more heavily when a card improves his hand. Occasionally, however, players will bluff. For example, take a player in hi-low seven-card stud who shows an ace and 2 and is betting confidently from the start. His next card is a 6. He bets the maximum again. His next card is a 4. Now his heavy bet convinces everyone that he has a perfect low hand. The 7 and 8 lows who are still in may very well drop. Showing the ace, 2, 6, and 4 is a perfect hand for bluffing a low, so that even if the player has paired up, he'll probably bet heavily, trying to drive the other lows out of the game.

Most players will bluff only when their cards show a strong hand. For this reason, you can be pretty sure that a player who shows nothing and bets heavily probably has a hidden good hand. He's not betting to get you out of the game. He's betting because he thinks he has the winning hand. Of course, you've got to fill in these general guidelines with experience. You may find a player in your group who only bluffs when his cards indicate garbage; or some players decide to bluff right from the beginning. Others only do it at the end when they didn't catch what they were going for. Others base their decision on the relative strength showing in the hands around them. This is why you've constantly got to check out your predictions against what actually happens, and modify your procedures to fit the individual players.

Let's look at some sample hands and see how betting and card reading can be combined to give more information:

Seven-Card Stud, Hi-Low

Player:	1	2	3	4	5	6
Card 1	(down)	(down)	(down)	(down)	(down)	(down)
Card 2	(down)	(down)	(down)	(down)	(down)	(down)
Card 3	4♠	6♠	J♣	Q♦	9♠	8♠
				*check	check	check
	bet $2†	call	call	call	call	fold

*high player on board will henceforth be noted with an asterisk, with no footnote.

†bets of $1, $2, $5 allowed at any time, three raises maximum, sandbagging allowed.

In this game of seven-card stud hi-low, flushes and straights count high only, so the best low is A, 2, 3, 4, 6, of different suits.

In the first round of betting, the high hand on board, player #4, checks. Players #5 and #6 check also, but player #1 bets $2. The other players then call except for player #6, who folds. This would indicate player #1 is probably going for a low hand and has three good low cards.

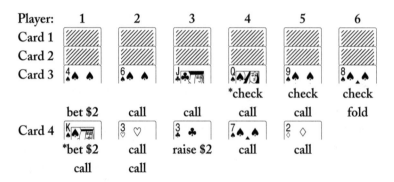

In the second round of betting, player #1 bets $2 again. With a 4♠ and K♠ showing, this could mean he's going for spades or that he still feels confident with his three low cards. Player #2 calls, indicating that the 3 and 6 showing have probably been building a good low, but not strong enough to raise on. When player #3 raises with a J♣ and 3♣ showing, we think he probably has four clubs, although he possibly could have three to a low, and possibly both. Player #4 calls with the Q♠ and 7♠ showing, indicating he may have three or four spades, or is looking for a low. Player #5 calls with a 9♠ and 2♦, indicating most likely a low.

Player:	1	2	3	4	5	6
Card 1	////	////	////	////	////	////
Card 2	////	////	////	////	////	////
Card 3	4♠ ♠	6♠ ♠	J♣	Q♠	9♠ ♠	8♠ ♠
				*check	check	check
	bet $2	call	call	call	call	fold
Card 4	K♠	3 ♡	3 ♣	7♠ ♠	2 ♢	
	*bet $2	call	raise $2	call	call	
	call	call				
Card 5	6♡ ♡	5♣ ♣	4♡ ♡	10♠ ♠	Q♢	
	*bet $5	call	call	call	fold	

In the third round, player #1 bets $5. Since his bet has gone up after receiving a 6♥, we can assume he's betting on the strength of his low hand, not spades. Player #2 calls, with three low cards showing. Player #3 doesn't raise this time. Since he was just dealt the 4♥, we can assume he was probably going for clubs and the heart didn't help. Player #4 calls after getting another spade. We can assume he's going for spades but is worried about player #3's clubs. Player #5 folds.

Player:	1	2	3	4	5	6
Card 1	(face down)	(face down)	(face down)	(face down)	(face down)	(face down)
Card 2	(face down)	(face down)	(face down)	(face down)	(face down)	(face down)
Card 3	4♠	6♠	J♣	Q♠	9♠	8♠
				*check	check	check
	bet $2	call	call	call	call	fold
Card 4	K♠	3♡	3♣	7♠	2♢	
	*bet $2	call	raise $2	call	call	
	call	call				
Card 5	6♡	5♣	4♡	10♠	Q♢	
	*bet $5	call	call	call	fold	
Card 6	Q♣	A♡	10♡	J♠		
		*bet $5	call	raise $5		
	raise $1	raise $5	call	call		
	call					

After the sixth card is dealt, we see the players as follows: player #1 is showing two spades and two low cards. The best he can have is four spades or 4 to a low, and he's probably going for the low, since he was betting from the first round. Player #2 is now showing four good low cards, indicating he probably has his low hand already, since he must have had something good down in order to stay in in the first place (although he could have paired up since). Player #3 shows two clubs and two hearts and two low cards. We figure he's probably going for a club flush, since he was betting when the clubs came out, but stopped since. Player #4 shows four spades. There's a good chance he has five spades, although he checked initially and has not yet raised a bet.

In the fourth round of betting the picture becomes clearer. Player #2 bets $5, indicating he probably does have his low hand. Player #3 calls, indicating he wants to try for the club flush on the last card. Player #4 raises $5, showing he already has his spade flush. Player #1 then raises $1, indicating he's determined to stay in for the last card, but wants to keep the money as low as possible. Player #2 takes the last raise for $5, having the best low hand at that moment. The rest of the players call.

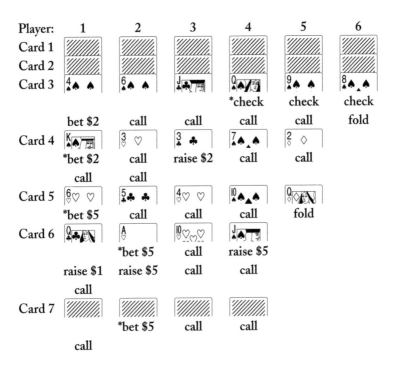

Now let's turn up the down cards and see what the results actually were:

Player:	1	2	3	4	5	6
Card 1	A♣	8♦	10♣	A♠	2♣	7♦
Card 2	2♠	4♦	K♣	2♥	3♦	J♥
Card 3	4♠	6♠	J♣	Q♠	9♠	8♠
				*check	check	check
	bet $2	call	call	call	call	fold
Card 4	K♠	3♥	3♣	7♠	2♦	
	*bet $2	call	raise $2	call	call	
	call	call				
Card 5	6♥	5♣	4♥	10♠	Q♦	
	*bet $5	call	call	call	fold	
Card 6	Q♣	A	10♥	J♠		
		*bet $5	call	raise $5		
	raise $1	raise $5	call	call		
	call					
Card 7	7♣	7♥	4♣	6♦		
		*bet $5	call	call		
	call					
	LOW	LOW	HIGH	HIGH		
		*bet $5	call	call		
	call					
		Winner		*Winner*		

Player #1 got a 7 on the last card, making his best low
7–6–4–2–A. Player #2 got a 7, but already had the winning low
of 6–5–4–3–A. Player #3 got a 4♣, giving him a club flush, king
high. Player #4 got a 6♦, but didn't need it since he already had
an ace high spade flush. Player #2 bets $5. Player #3 simply calls
because he's pretty certain player #4 has a spade flush, and he
hasn't seen the A♠. Player #4 calls because he figures player #3
may have caught his club flush, and possibly the ace. Player #1
calls, knowing that player #2 probably has him beat for low, but
there's a chance he's bluffing on the good show cards. It won't
cost player #1 any more than the $5 to find out. Players #2 and
#4 split the pot.

Here's an example from five-card stud:

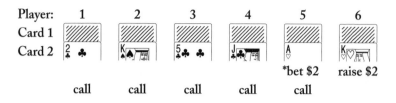

In the first round of betting, player #5 bets $2 on his ace. We figure he probably just has the ace. When player #6 raises $2 we wonder if he has something better than a king high, say a pair of kings, or possibly an ace in the hole. The other players call, indicating there are probably no pairs.

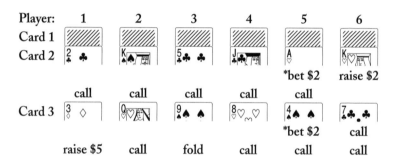

After the third card is dealt it doesn't look like any of the hands have improved much. But the betting proves otherwise. This time when player #5 bets $2, player #6 doesn't raise, indicating he probably doesn't have a pair of kings. Then player #1 raises $5, showing he must have caught a pair of 3s. Player #2 calls, #3 drops, and the rest call.

Player:	1	2	3	4	5	6
Card 1	/////	/////	/////	/////	/////	/////
Card 2	2♣	K♠	5♣	J♠	A♡	K♡
					*bet $2	raise $2
	call	call	call	call	call	
Card 3	3♢	Q♡	9♠	8♡	4♠	7♣
					*bet $2	call
	raises $5	call	fold	call	call	call
Card 4	A♠	10♢		8♣	K♢	7♠
				*bet $5	call	call
	call	raise $5		call	call	call
	call					

The fourth card gives two players pairs showing, #4 and #6. Player #4 bets with a pair of 8s showing. Player #5 calls, probably hoping to pair up his king or ace on the last card. Player #6 calls with the pair of 7s, hoping for two pair or three of a kind on the last card. Player #1 calls for the same reason. But the surprise comes when player #2 raises $5 indicating the 10 he just got must have paired up with is hole card. He figures he's the highest hand with a pair of 10s. The other players call.

Player:	1	2	3	4	5	6
Card 1	3♣	10♡	6♣	2♠	6♡	A♦
Card 2	2♣	K♠	5♣	J♣	A♡	K♡
					*bet $5	raise $2
	call	call	call	call	call	
Card 3	3♦	Q♡	9♠	8♡	4♠	7♣
					*bet $2	call
	raise $5	call	fold	call	call	call
Card 4	A♠	10♦		8♣	K♦	7♠
				*bet $5	call	call
	call	raise $5		call	call	call
	call					
Card 5	10♠	6♠		A♠	4♡	7♦
						*bet $5
	fold	fold		fold	fold	Winner

The fifth card makes an obvious winner, player #6 with three 7s. But looking at the hole cards now, we see that player #1 did have a pair of 3s, player #2 had a pair of 10s, and player #6 was raising initially on his ace in the hole.

When you're reading the cards in a player's hand, be sure to take into account any changes in his betting. A card that may look insignificant taken on face value might prove to be just the opposite if a player bets out heavily or raises after receiving it.

Peeking

Poker experts say that when you're dealt your cards in stud you should take one look at your hole card or cards, memorize them, and not look at them again. Many players, however, don't follow this rule. Some study their hole cards every time they're dealt another card. It's as if they need to *see* the cards in order to figure out what they've got.

Other players will only peek at their hole cards on special occasions—for example, when they are very good. These players need to check periodically to make sure the cards are really what they thought they were. The stimulus for them to peek might be another player's large bet, for example. Before they call or raise, they peek to make sure they really do have that great hand.

The next time you play, observe the peeking habits of the other players. Which players constantly look at their hole cards? Which ones never peek except under certain circumstances? Try to predict whether their peeking is due to very good hole cards, or because the cards were so *un*interesting that they couldn't remember them.

Showing

Do any of the players in your game show their cards to non-players, or players who have dropped? Some players show their cards all the time. They don't mind letting a player who has folded see their hand. Sometimes a folded player will ask, "Can I see what you've got?" This routine revealing of a hand doesn't tell much, unless the looker gives something away by his expression, or exceptional interest in the outcome of a game he was previously disinterested in.

But when a player who normally doesn't show his hand asks someone to take a look, then it does mean something. One night in draw poker, Doug, an occasional player in our game, came up with a fantastic hand. I knew it was fantastic because the guy couldn't resist showing it to everybody who had folded.

Some people will do this when they have rotten luck. Say in hi-low draw they keep four low hearts and draw one card. When they get a K♠, they want to share their disappointment by showing what they caught to a sympathetic non-player.

The player who gets a straight flush or four of a kind in a game without wild cards will often be dying to share his phenomenal luck with someone. While some can exercise self-control and save it for the end of the game when they're raking in the chips, you should be aware of those players who can't contain themselves. Make sure you know who they are and watch out when they start showing a hand around and betting heavy at the same time.

Picking Up

There are occasions for picking up cards in draw, replacements in stud games, or the pass in pass games such as Anaconda.** Most players develop regular picking-up habits. Some like to take their draw cards in draw poker and mix them up with the rest of their hand, then squeeze them out one by one. Some players pick up all their replace or pass cards at once. Others leave the cards on the table and pick them up one at a time.

The thing to watch for is when somebody does something different, like "forgetting" to pick up their draw or pass cards, or only picking up some of them. We were playing Anaconda one night and had just finished the first pass of three cards. Joey bet $5. Then Dave said to him, "Joey, don't you want your pass cards?" Joey had neglected to pick up the three cards, yet he was betting $5. The prediction was that he had four of a kind already, and that's exactly what he had.

Now Dave has a big mouth. He could have shut up and kept the information to himself. Eventually Joey would probably have noticed the three cards and picked them up. But by drawing attention to it, Dave let everybody know Joey had the four of a kind.

Another thing to watch out for is where the draw cards are placed in a hand. For example, if a player keeps four cards and draws one, where does he place that card—in the middle, at the right, or at the left? Some players like to put the card where it "belongs," that is, in its proper place in a straight, flush, or low hand. If more than one card is picked up, how does the player move them around in his hand? Does he just pick them up and leave them in one place, or move them around, positioning them? You'll have to observe a player's habits in this area a number of times, again matching your prediction with actual hands at the end of the game.

**This is a hi-low game. Seven cards are dealt to each player. There's a pass of three cards to the left (or right), a bet, another pass of two cards, a bet, another pass of one card, a bet, then a rollover of the first four cards with betting after each card is turned over.

Touching

Have you ever noticed a player nervously fondling his up cards in stud poker? Sometimes a person will unconsciously touch a couple of cards while he's thinking about the possibilities. If he always touches his cards indiscriminately, this won't help much. But it may be that he's resting his finger on the 3♠ because he's got two 3s in the hole, and dreaming about getting four, or a full house.

Other players will try to hide their good cards. They'll keep their cards out of view behind an ashtray, an arm, or a candy dish, hoping that no one will notice what a good hand they have. While some may deliberately do this, it's usually unconscious. The important being for you to do is notice what's going on.

George, a graduate student, is a basically nervous kind of guy to start with. He's always fingering his cards, but when they really look good, he tends to surround them with a stack of chips on one side and his arm on the other. Steve is always yelling at George because he can't see George's cards. This makes George more nervous and he usually knocks over a stack of chips in the process. Of course, all of this draws even more attention to George's good hand, but he never seems to learn.

Another example of touching is when a player acts possessive of his hole cards, or his whole hand in draw poker. A player who normally may not touch his hole cards, or lay down his hand in draw and not look at it, may suddenly start to guard his cards for dear life when he's got something special. He gets a little paranoid and thinks if he doesn't hold on to them tightly, they'll disappear or change into something else. So watch out for this act at your table.

Those Hidden Good Hands

While the hidden good hand is next to impossible to read from the cards alone, interpreting signs of betting, peeking, showing, and touching can help. As, of course, will your analysis of that person as a player in general, and how he acts in specific situations (see Chapters 2 and 3). But let's see if there's anything at all the cards *can* tell you about hidden good hands.

Player:	1	2	3	4	5	6
Card 1	▨	▨	▨	▨	▨	▨
Card 2	▨	▨	▨	▨	▨	▨
Card 3	7♠	10♡	10♣	4♢	6♣	J♡
Card 4	7♡	9♡	K♠	2♢	3♠	A♢
Card 5	7♢	5♡	5♣	8♣	9♢	5♢
Card 6	5♠	A♡	9♣	8♡	6♡	K♣
Card 7	▨	▨	▨	▨	▨	▨

In this game, player #6 has the hidden good hand. But how do you know it? For one thing, he's staying in on all bets, in spite of the heavy opposition: player #1 shows three 7s; player #2 shows four hearts; player #3 shows three clubs, player #4 shows two 8s; player #5 shows a pair of 6s, and all of these players are not only staying in, but betting heavily. So why is player #6 in? What could he possibly have? His flush possibilities aren't good, because he has only two diamonds showing, and five are up on the board. It's doubtful he would be in for a straight or three of a kind, since player #2 may be likely to have a flush. So he must be going for a full house or four of a kind. What could he have in the hole? Looking around the board, we see three other 5s up, so we know he can't have 5s paired. Checking out the jacks, we don't see any others, so it's likely he's paired or tripled jacks. There's one other king showing, and one ace, so these have possibilities also. The fact that he stays in the betting, and then raises after the last card, indicates he probably caught a high full house. When we turn up all the down cards, we see that that's exactly what he has, a full house with jacks and aces.

Player:	1	2	3	4	5	6
Card 1	3 ♥	4♥ ♥	2 ♣	3 ♦	2 ♥	J♦
Card 2	8♠ ♠	Q♠	2 ♠	6♦ ♦	6♠ ♠	A♣
Card 3	7♠ ♠	10♥ ♥	10♣ ♣	4♦ ♦	6♣ ♣	J♥
Card 4	7♥ ♥	9♥ ♥	K♠	2 ♦	3 ♠	A♦
Card 5	7♦ ♦	5♥ ♥	5♣ ♣	8♣ ♣	9♦ ♦	5♦ ♦
Card 6	5♠ ♠	A♥	9♣ ♣	8♥ ♥	6♥ ♥	K♠
Card 7	3 ♣	8♦ ♦	Q♥	9♠ ♠	Q♦	J♠

Player #1 came in second with a full house, 7s up, and player #2 came in third with a heart flush. Reading the cards at least indicated that player #6's high full house was very possible. If we had seen a lot of jacks, aces, and kings up on the board, we could have suspected a possible bluff. However, with all the good cards showing in the other hands, it would be unlikely for him to attempt to bluff that kind of competition.

Let's look at another situation:

Seven-Card Stud, Hi-Low

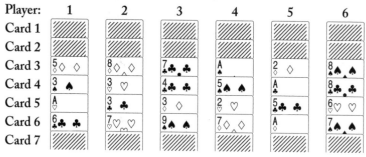

Player:	1	2	3	4	5	6
Card 1	▨	▨	▨	▨	▨	▨
Card 2	▨	▨	▨	▨	▨	▨
Card 3	5♦ ♦	8♦ ♦	7♣ ♣	A♠	2♦ ♦	8♠ ♠
Card 4	3 ♠	3 ♥	4♣ ♣	5♠ ♠	A♣	8♣ ♣
Card 5	A♥	3♣ ♣	3♦ ♦	2 ♥	5♣ ♣	6♥ ♥
Card 6	6♣ ♣	7♥ ♥	9♠ ♠	7♦ ♦	A♦	7♠ ♠
Card 7	▨	▨	▨	▨	▨	▨

Looking at the four up cards in each hand, these are the possibilities we see: player #1 has four good low cards, a low straight possibility, no flush possibilities. Player #2 has a pair of 3s and two hearts toward a flush. Player #3 has three cards for a low, and two clubs for a flush. Player #4 has four cards to a low and two spades. Player #5 has a pair of aces, three cards for a low, and two clubs or two diamonds to a flush. Player #6 has a pair of 8s and three cards to a straight, or two spades to a flush. Players #1, #3, #4, and #5 could easily be going for lows since they all have three or four cards to a low showing. Player #5 with the pair of aces could also be going high. We look around and see that the other two aces are showing, one 2 is showing, and two 5s are showing. This means he has no chance for three aces, but could have two pair, and might get a full house with 2s or 5s up.

Player #2 doesn't look like he's going low because he's doubled up on 3s and shows a 7 and 8. Most of the low cards he would need for a hidden low hand are showing: all the aces, two 2s, one 4, three 5s, and two 6s. So we decide he must be going for high. What could he have? His other two 3s are out. Two of his 8s are showing. The other three 7s are showing. He doesn't have much to indicate a straight, but he has two hearts and there are only three other hearts up on the board, indicating a chance he may have them hidden. We figure he probably has two hearts in the hole and is going for a flush.

Player #6 doesn't indicate a low, but he has 6, 7, 8 toward a straight. Since we see only one 9 and no 10s showing, we figure he might have it. There are one 6, three 7s, and one 8 showing elsewhere, which indicate poor possibilities for three of a kind or a full house. We bet on the straight.

Turning all the cards up now, we see that our prediction about player #2 was correct. He had a hidden flush:

Player:	1	2	3	4	5	6
Card 1	9 ◊	K ♥	4 ♠	4 ♡	Q ♣	6 ♠
Card 2	2 ♠	8 ♡	6 ◊	J ♥	2 ♣	K ◊
Card 3	5 ◊	8 ◊	7 ♣	A ♠	2 ◊	8 ♠
Card 4	3 ♠	3 ♡	4 ♣	5 ♠	A ♠	8 ♣
Card 5	A ♠	3 ♣	3 ◊	2 ♡	5 ♣	6 ♡
Card 6	6 ♣	7 ♡	9 ♠	7 ◊	A ♠	7 ♠
Card 7	4 ◊	9 ♡	Q ♥	10 ♠	J ◊	J ♠

But player #6 had two pair, 6s and 8s, and was unable to catch for a full house. Player #5 had possibilities with two pair and four to a flush, but didn't catch. Players #1, #3, and #4 were going for lows, as we suspected, and player #1 won with a 6–4–3–2–A.

Reading cards can tell you what the possibilities are for each player. When you figure out the possible hands a player might be going for, check around to see how many of their required cards are already out. This helps you decide the *probabilities*. By adding betting data, you get information about a player's evaluation of his strength, and the importance of each new card—for good or bad. Finally, be alert to telling signs when players peek, show, touch, and pick up their cards.

Reading Players, General

AFTER YOU PLAY with a group for a while, you'll begin to notice the same people showing the same playing styles week after week. People play poker for all kinds of reasons: to pass the time; to prove how smart they are; to gamble; to make money; to lose money; to socialize; to belong to the group; to get away from home; to drink; to eat; to get attention ... you name it. But a person who's a gambler one week will probably be a gambler the next. There's usually one overall primary motivation that brings a player back every week.

However, no one will admit their primary motivation. They're not going to say, "I go to poker every week because that's the only place where I belong, where I don't feel alienated, where I can just be me and nobody cares." Or, "It's an excuse to eat and drink and smoke—I couldn't care less whether I win or lose." The chronic loser can't say, "I go to poker without fail every week, and every week I lose, so obviously I must *want* to lose or I'd quit."

So—everybody plays poker to *win*. No matter what their primary reason for playing is, if you asked them whether they were trying to win or not, they'd laugh at you. Everybody plays poker to win. With this conscious goal to win in mind, each player develops his own winning strategy, whether it involves mathematical computations, memorized systems, intuition, or courting Lady Luck.

Now we've got two things to find out about each player: his primary motivation for playing, and his conscious "strategy to win." The third controlling factor is the group's motivation, or influence over players. For example, some groups stress the social or fun aspect of a game. Penny-ante games are generally always played with this goal in mind—by keeping the stakes low, no one will get hurt, and everybody can just have fun. Other groups enjoy the thrill of risk—they play for relatively high stakes (relative to the income of the players). In these games, a big loser can end up short on food or rent money. A big winner can surprise his family with a new TV or special vacation.

The fourth factor we're going to look at in this chapter is the effect of external conditions and other situations that change a player's normal mode of operation. These include reactions to heat, cold, smoke, lateness of the hour, as well as specific reactions of a player to drink, personal problems, and the tone of the conversation.

Since you're reading this book, I assume you're a player who's serious about winning. So let's analyze the above factors and see how they can help you do this.

Primary Motivation

I lived in a university town and most of the players in our group were connected with the college—professor, graduate students, and staff. A few worked in local business or industry. Our regular group originally consisted of five people: Dave, a law student, organized the group originally. While he was a consistent, although not big, winner, making money was not his prime motivation. The game offered him prestige and an ego boost—here were men who thought they were a lot smarter than Dave losing to him every week. Playing the all-knowing parent, he would often give the other players tips on how to play better. He took as his understudy Steve, a hyperactive graduate student. Steve and Dave met before each game to discuss various strategies. When Steve made a smart play, he'd look to Dave for recognition. When he had a bad night, he'd confess his errors to Dave, looking for guidance and support. So Steve's prime motivation was to show us (mostly Dave) what a clever, good boy he was. He wanted attention, love, and praise from the group and pulled all kinds of antics to get this.

Mike was the big gambler in the group. A professor of business administration, he was an aggressive risk-taker, going for the long shots on his lucky nights and bluffing the hell out of us when he wasn't so lucky. His biggest thrill was putting one over on us.

Joey played to have a good time. He enjoyed the verbal repartee, making jokes, observing the game, eating, and seeing how the cards came out. That was his weak point—always wanting to be in the play and see what cards he'd get. He liked to play so much that he didn't get out soon enough or often enough.

Tom was our toughest player. He was tough because no one could figure him out. He'd sit there all night downing one beer after another, puffing on his cigar, saying nothing. He never got involved in any arguments, or showed any emotion one way or another, winning or losing. You'd never notice he was there, except at the end of the evening when he was likely to be the big winner.

Our occasional players came for various reasons. Doug and Paul, also professors, came for a "night out with the boys" once or twice a month. Nervous George, a graduate student, came fairly regularly, but got so embarrassed every time he lost more than two dollars that he'd stay away for a while before coming back.

Take a look at the players in your group. Why do you think each of them comes every week? What kind of satisfaction are they getting out of it? See if you can pin down the prime motivation for each player.

Strategy for Winning

Okay, let's see how these prime motivations affect each player's actions, and consequently his strategy for winning. I said that Dave equated consistent winning with superiority. It enabled him to stand tall and be the all-knowing parent, dispensing an occasional tidbit of wisdom to the group. Since he had so few real feelings of self-worth, his superiority at the poker table was very important to him. He developed such a tight position that a heavy loss would have been devastating to him. Therefore he guardedly developed a very conservative play. He folded early and often, waiting for the perfect hand before putting his money on the table. He bluffed only often enough to prove he was capable of doing it, and only when the situation offered a high probability of success. His methods worked best against players who were unaware of his style, and so he exploited newcomers to the fullest. We all watched him take a new player to the slaughter many times. The rest of us knew, however, that when Dave was betting, you could be pretty sure he had it. So we got out. When the game first started, Dave was a big winner. Until we got on to him. He still continued to win, but not as much.

Steve's play wasn't as simple as Dave's. Steve was more erratic—full of fancy, one-of-a-kind creations designed to win the admiration of the group, and especially of Dave. Sometimes Steve would get into a style and stick with it for a while, like "build the pot, win or not." During that period we could count on Steve to bet out early in the game, no matter what cards he held. One thing we could be sure of is that his thinking would invariably be complex—he'd never take the simple route to a problem's solution. Instead of double-think, he'd use triple-think and often as not end up screwing himself because of it. So with Steve, we had to be ever-alert to his latest patterns, and expect the bizarre. Sometimes, I suspected Dave of manipulating Steve to his own interests, because inevitably Dave was the one who seemed to benefit from Steve's gyrations.

While we could be pretty sure Dave wasn't bluffing ninety-five percent of the time, with Mike, you never knew. He could be bluffing at any time. Then again, he could be having a lucky night and hitting the long shots. Mike often pulled his stunts on newcomers, too, and when one outfoxed him he'd turn sullen and argumentative. Other times he'd sit in moody silence, playing more conservatively for a while until a change in luck picked up his mood again. When he walked in high, you could be sure he was going to be taking big risks and loving the whole thing.

Joey wasn't really a bad poker player when he was trying to play good poker. But as I said above, he'd stay in more often and longer than he should because he liked to play and wanted to see what cards he was going to get. So you could count on him to put a chip in when he didn't really have the hand to do it with. You didn't have to worry about scaring him out with a bet for a round or two. He'd contribute to the pot in order to play.

Tom, as I said, was tough. He was a good reader and wasn't afraid to fold three of a kind if he was pretty sure he was beaten by a full house. He had a good sense of what was happening around the table. This was useful information to have. When I saw Tom dropping out with decent cards showing, I had to ask, what did he see that made him fold? So I used Tom as an indicator of what was happening.

Most players choose a winning strategy that will complement their primary motive for playing. Someone who enjoys the risks and excitement will obviously try for the long shots, want to be in the big pots, and bluff. Players who look for the social aspects—eating, drinking, small talk, camaraderie—will probably not pay as much attention to their game. They may intuitively develop some good playing habits, but they're not going to engage in a lot of critical analysis, heavy concentration, and manipulative strategies. They're likely to be a bit loose in their play, and not care about or notice occasional bad plays.

The player who's trying to prove how smart he is will be very concerned about his strategy, and how his play looks to the rest of the group. He'll probably be critical of others' play, discuss strategy, and give advice. He won't be likely to drink if drinking makes him foggy. He'll probably be somewhat tight and compulsive, and always watching to grade himself on how well he's done and to compare his skill with that of the rest of the group. Winning in itself isn't *that* important to him, except that he knows in poker if you lose consistently it's because of bad playing, not bad luck. In fact, during his own streaks of bad luck he has to constantly reinforce his ego that it's luck and not his playing that made him lose. During a long losing period he goes through a lot of soul-searching.

Players with a mathematical bent will often use these skills to show how smart they are. They'll spout probabilities at you all the time. "Dope! Couldn't you see that with four spades showing you had a one in eight chance of making your flush, when Charlie had a one in three chance of making his straight!" It really drives these guys crazy when somebody makes a one in seventy-five chance hand and beats them out of a fifty dollar pot.

To see how knowing the primary motivation and winning strategy of each player can help your decision-making during a game, let's look at a sample hand:

Seven-Card Stud, Hi-Low

(bets $1, $2, and $5 any time, maximum three raises)

	Dave	Mike	Steve	Tom	Joey	Me
Card 1						K◇
Card 2						A◇
Card 3	5♣	7♡	K♠	9◇	10♡	6◇
			*bet $5	call	call	call
	call	call				

In the first round Steve bets $5. Everyone calls up to me. With three diamonds and two cards to a low, including the ace, I call also. Dave and Mike call in turn.

	Dave	Mike	Steve	Tom	Joey	Me
Card 1						K◇
Card 2						A◇
Card 3	5♣	7♡	K♠	9◇	10♡	6◇
			*bet $5	call	call	call
	call	call				
Card 4	Q♣	4♠	2♡	Q♠	8♣	7◇
			*bet $5	fold	call	call
	call	raise $5	call		call	call
	call					

On the second round Steve is still high on board and bets another $5. Since it's Steve betting the $5 each time, I don't take it too seriously. Tom drops. Joey and I call. I considered raising, since I now have four diamonds and three good low cards, but I simply call to see what Dave and Mike are going to do. Dave calls. Mike raises $5. The rest of us call the raise. With the 7♥ and 4♠ showing, I figure Mike is going for low and is letting us know he's confident. I'm not worried much about Steve and Joey. They don't show much and they haven't indicated a lot of confidence. But Dave worries me. For him to be in on these $5 bets and raises, he must have a pretty good hand. Yet he's showing the 5♣ and Q♣. I wonder if he's going for a flush.

	Dave	Mike	Steve	Tom	Joey	Me
Card 1	▨	▨	▨	▨	▨	K◇
Card 2	▨	▨	▨	▨	▨	A◇
Card 3	5♣	7♡	K♠	9◇	10♡	6◇
			*bet $5	call	call	call
	call	call				
Card 4	Q♠	4♠	2♡	Q♠	8♣	7◇
			*bet $5	fold	call	call
	call	raise $5	call		call	call
	call					
Card 5	3♡	10◇	5◇		6♡	Q♡
			*check		check	check
	bet $5	call	fold		call	call

On the third round, Steve checks, indicating his hand isn't going anywhere. Joey checks. Since the Q♥ didn't help me, I check also. Dave bets $5, making me think he's probably going for low and has four good cards although I'm still not positive he's not going for the flush. Mike didn't improve his low hand with the 10♦, but he calls. Steve folds. Joey calls, and I wonder what on earth he's going for with a 10♥, an 8♣, and a 6♥. He must be going high, but for what? A heart flush? A straight? I simply call.

	Dave	Mike	Steve	Tom	Joey	Me
Card 1	/////	/////	/////	/////	/////	K♦
Card 2	/////	/////	/////	/////	/////	A♦
Card 3	5♣	7♥	K♠	9♦	10♥	6♦
			*bet $5	call	call	call
	call	call				
Card 4	Q♠	4♠	2♥	Q♠	8♣	7♦
			*bet $5	fold	call	call
	call	raise $5	call		call	call
	call					
Card 5	3♥	10♦	5♦		6♥	Q♥
			*check		check	check
	bet $5	call	fold		call	call
Card 6	6♠	7♠			9♣	3♦
		*bet $5			call	call
	raise $5	raise $5			raise $1	call
	call	call				

On the next round Mike is high with a pair of 7s. He bets $5.
I figure he must be working on a high hand, and probably doesn't
have it yet. Joey calls. With the 6–8–9–10, I figure he must be
going for a straight. The flush I caught with the 3 ♦ will beat that.
But will it beat whatever Mike's got? I've got a feeling Mike's
bluffing—that he's hoping to knock Joey out and then be the only
one going for high to win half the pot. Mike raises another $5,
which confirms my belief that he's trying to get Joey out and con-
vince me to go low. Joey raises $1, the last raise. The rest of us all
call around.

	Dave	Mike	Steve	Tom	Joey	Me
Card 1						K◇
Card 2						A◇
Card 3	5♣	7♥	K♠ *bet $5	9◇ call	10♥ call	6◇ call
	call	call				
Card 4	Q♣	4♠	2♥ *bet $5	Q♠ fold	8♣ call	7◇ call
	call	raise $5	call		call	call
	call					
Card 5	3♥	10◇	5◇ *check		6♥ check	Q♥ check
	bet $5	call	fold		call	call
Card 6	6♠	7♠ *bet $5			9♣ call	3◇ call
	raise $5	raise $5			raise $1	call
	call	call				
Card 7	(hidden)	(hidden) *bet $5			(hidden) call	4♥ raise $5
	raise $5	raise $5			call	call
	call					

My last card is a 4♥. I now have a 7–6–4–3–A low or an ace high diamond flush. What should I do? First, the betting. Mike bets $5 again, but he'd have to no matter what he caught, to keep up the front. Joey calls. Did he get his straight or is he hoping we'll all go low, or what? I raise $5 to see how Dave reacts to this. He raises another $5. Mike takes the last raise for $5 and the rest of us all call.

Now to declare high or low. Looking at Mike's possibilities, he *could* have a full house, with only one 7 showing, one 4 in my hand, and one 10 showing. But his initial call on the first round, and his bet on the 4♠, tell me he was originally going for low and backed into a high bluff at the end of the game. Even if Mike or Joey caught a flush by some fluke, mine is bound to be higher with the ace-king. I'm also certain Dave has a 6–5 low, which would beat mine, so I declare high. Mike and Joey also declare high and Dave declares low.

	Dave	Mike	Steve	Tom	Joey	Me
Card 1						K◇
Card 2						A◇
Card 3	5♣	7♥	K♠	9♦	10♥	6♦
			*bet $5	call	call	call
	call	call				
Card 4	Q♣	4♠	2♥	Q♠	8♣	7♦
			*bet $5	fold	call	call
	call	raise $5	call		call	call
	call					
Card 5	3♥	10♦	5♦		6♥	Q♥
			*check		check	check
	bet $5	call	fold		call	call
Card 6	6♠	7♠			9♣	3♦
		*bet $5			call	call
	raise $5	raise $5			raise $1	call
	call	call				
Card 7	(hidden)	(hidden)			(hidden)	4♥
		*bet $5			call	raise $5
	raise $5	raise $5			call	call
	call				call	
	LOW	HIGH			HIGH	HIGH
	**bet $5	raise $5			fold	call
	raise $5	fold				call

**Being the only one to call low, Dave is the first better.

Dave bets $5. Mike raises $5 (to scare me and Joey). Joey drops (he was hoping to be the only one going high). I call. Dave raises $5. Mike drops. Dave and I split the pot. Here's how all the hands looked:

	Dave	Mike	Steve	Tom	Joey	Me
Card 1	A♠	5♠	8♦	A♠	J♠	K♦
Card 2	2♣	3♠	5♥	3♣	J♦	A♦
Card 3	5♣	7♥	K♠	9♦	10♥	6♦
Card 4	Q♣	4♠	2♥	Q♠	8♣	7♦
Card 5	3♥	10♦	5♦		6♥	Q♥
Card 6	6♠	7♠			9♣	3♦
Card 7	Q♦	9♥			10♣	4♥

Poker Groups

There have been a lot of studies done on groups—how they form, how leaders emerge, how individual members influence and are influenced by the group. The basic heading for these theories is "Organizational Behavior." It's interesting how people act in a group, and how the group becomes an entity in itself. Coalitions may form. One or more members may become trouble-makers, attempting to disrupt the group or change the rules by which it works. One person usually takes on the position of arbitrator, attempting to smooth out conflicts and keep the group together.

These patterns can be seen around the poker table. Usually there's an "in" group of regular players who develop rules and the style of playing the group will adopt. New players and irregulars are expected to adapt to the group's mode of operation. For example, if the group doesn't like wild cards, they'll give a new player a hard time if he tries to introduce wild cards into the game. The group's leader will tell the new person what he thinks, and the other members of the group will back him up.

In order for a new player to have influence over the group and introduce new rules or styles of playing, he'll have to first win over some of the old members and form his own coalition. When he's gathered sufficient strength, he can begin to introduce his own ideas and get some of them accepted. He may even eventually work his way into a leadership position.

A poker group usually has many rules that are based solely on a matter of habit. A new player may ask, "Can't we change that rule? I don't like it." Or, "I don't think it's fair." The answer will be, "This is the way we always play." For example, in our group the last person to raise is the bettor in draw poker. Other groups may play so that the first person who bet out the previous round is the bettor, regardless of any raises. Neither rule is especially better or fairer than the other, but if a new player comes in and suggests a change, he'll receive a lot of opposition.

Group Influence

Every group has a primary reason for being. If your poker group's prime motivation is to provide an opportunity for social interaction, every member will be influenced to be sociable. There will be little emphasis on who wins or who loses, on who is the better player, on getting the cards mixed efficiently so that the next hand can be played immediately. Members will be encouraged to "have a good time," to engage in small talk, to eat and drink, to "be good sports," to overlook errors in dealing, to give the other fellow the benefit of the doubt. The game is merely an excuse for friends to get together and have a good time.

In such a group you may find it difficult to enforce standard playing procedures. For example, if you try to make a rule that every player in at the end of the hand must show his cards, you may find it a difficult one to carry out. Players who don't care may throw their cards in, not remembering the rule. You may be asked what you had when you weren't in until the end, and considered a poor sport if you refuse to answer. Players may bet out of turn, forget how many raises there are left, and similar sloppy behavior. If you try to make them pay attention and play a serious game, you may find resentment and dislike for your efforts. If you're really interested in trying to play winning poker, I suggest you find another group, or adapt to this group. You can actually use their carelessness to advantage, as long as you're not obnoxious and obvious about it. For example, when they ask you what cards you had, lie. Be patient and helpful rather than demanding and short-tempered. It could pay off in the end.

40

Another group may be interested in a high-risk game where they can gamble with their rent money. They're the types that double the stakes on the last hand, make a lot of side bets, and choose games that will make big pots. They don't like tight players, and bluffing is their favorite pastime. This group will often play for table stakes. While the members of this group are usually big courters of luck, they can also be pretty shrewd players, so it's advisable to join it prepared to take a loss the first few nights. You'll need to study their playing habits in order to predict well, and you'll have to ride with the group's mode of playing in order to be accepted by them.

My group was out to prove how smart they all were. While the actual money won or lost wasn't significant to most of the players, they took their game *very* seriously. There were always two decks of cards on the table and a system was used to make sure a deck was always shuffled and ready for the next dealer. The smallest issue that might come up during a game was discussed and voted on, with a rule set for the future. Some nights we spent more time arguing about procedure than we did playing.

Of course we had a rule that every player in until the end must show his cards. If a new player forgot to do this, he'd be interrogated until he showed *every* card in his hand. He wasn't allowed to simply say, "I had a straight." Or, "I didn't have anything." We even developed rules about who could kibitz during the game, and what kind of subjects were permissible in conversation.

New players were quickly indoctrinated into the serious style of our game. Anyone who didn't take it seriously, preferring small talk to dealing or betting, got such a put-down that he either became more serious or didn't return anymore. And anyone who lost regularly and heavily was made to feel—unless he was totally insensitive—what a schmuck he was.

Egos were built and broken in our game. Many of our players avidly read poker books, tried out hands before the game, and analyzed what happened after the game. Winning through cleverness, not luck, is what was important to them. Most of them refused to drink any alcohol during the game because it might slow down their thinking.

Such a group exerts a lot of pressure on its members. It was very tough for Joey, for example, to really have a good time playing. Joey didn't care about winning so much. He liked to play. But he found himself thought a fool by the others since he usually ended up a consistent loser. He eventually dropped out of the group.

Since this group didn't encourage anyone to have a good time, to feel okay about losing money, everyone played pretty conservatively; there wasn't much money going around. This wasn't a good group, therefore, in which to win a lot of money. But it was a good group in which to sharpen up one's poker skills.

What kind of a group do you play in? How can you use the group's style to your advantage? If you find yourself unable to adapt to a particular group, or find that you simply don't enjoy playing with them, look around for another group. Or, you might attempt influencing the group to change. But be aware of its influence on the game and on each player, including yourself.

External Conditions

Some people play poker all night long with the same intensity and alertness. Others get foggy with the late hour, especially if they've been drinking and eating a lot through the night. First you should find out what kind of a player you are. Does your play get better or worse late at night? Keep track of your winnings and losses hour by hour, for several weeks. When do you win the most, early or late in the evening? If you do well in the later hours, encourage your group to play later. If you do poorly, go home before you get tired. In order to avoid the group's anger, tell them ahead of time that you have to leave at a certain time.

If you require a snack to keep your strength up, and the host doesn't provide anything, bring a sandwich with you. Whenever we played at Dave's house he never served any food. By ten or eleven o'clock I was usually starving, so I began to bring a sandwich. I could tell that most of the guys were hungry too, but didn't think ahead enough to bring something.

Temperature is another issue. If you're too hot, you're likely to be groggy and not think as well. If you're too cold, you won't be able to concentrate either. Since you can't always count on your host and the other players to agree with you about opening a window or turning up a thermostat, it's best to allow yourself some options. Dress in something light and bring a sweater.

Smoke can be an irritant, but not something you can always do anything about. If smoke bothers you, ask to sit next to non-smokers, keep a window or vent open, etc. When you're sitting out a hand leave the room and get some fresh air.

In general, when you're feeling low you're likely to play poorly. Don't be afraid to leave early if you've got a bad headache or something else is bothering you. If you don't want to leave because it would break up the game, at least play more conservatively until you feel better.

Be observant of how other players are feeling. If you know Jack always plays looser when he's drinking a lot, use this information to help you predict his moves. All kinds of personal problems and moods can influence your own or other's play. Be aware of what's happening and use the information to help your game. I've noticed, for example, that Steve always plays better when he's angry or hurt. So when he tried his childish antics, I didn't oppose him as I had done in the beginning. I figured, let him have his way. That will keep him happy and he won't try so hard to win. He didn't mind losing when he was in a good mood.

Observe and Learn

To figure out what affects the players in your group, observe what they do, and what "turns them on." Pinpoint each player's primary motivation and how the group tends to facilitate it. Isolate the winning strategy adopted by the players and how it affects their play. Also be aware of external factors, and changes in personal situations and moods that have an effect on the individual and on the group.

Reading Players, Specific

EVERY PLAYER HAS HIS OWN individual quirks that he exhibits during a poker game. In order to interpret these signs, you've got to study the individual specifically. Does he suddenly sit up straighter when he's got a good hand? Does he yawn when he's got a mediocre hand? Knowing these kinds of things can help you predict more accurately, and thereby win more money.

Starting with the regular players in your group, begin to study their individual habits during a game. Pick one person and try to note everything you can about his behavior. Write everything down when you get home from the game. Then try to match the behavior with his cards, and keep track of the results. For example, if you see him scratching his head every now and then, try to match that behavior with the value of his cards. Does he do this only when he has a bad hand or when he has a good hand? Or does he scratch his head randomly throughout the evening simply because he has dandruff?

By isolating a player's habits that are consistent indicators, these signs will become as important to you (and perhaps more important) as a large bet or raise. Let's look at some of the areas you might begin to discover signals in the behavior of the players at your table.

Change in Voice

Ordinarily you may not be aware of voice changes. But many of us tend to speak in a higher pitch when we're excited or nervous. If we're angry, we may speak louder. If we're worried or preoccupied, we may speak more softly, or mumble.

Some players won't allow themselves to change their voice during a game. They control themselves by keeping their voice at the same pitch throughout the game. Many players, however, will unconsciously change their voice pitch or loudness, even if only slightly, in the proper motivating situation. Listen to your group at the next game. Do you hear anger rising in someone's voice when they come in second, missing out on a big pot? Watch the player whose voice suddenly goes up in pitch after he picks up his draw cards. Does he end up the winner at the end of the game? What did he draw?

Steve is a pretty excitable guy to start with. His normal voice is loud and quite expressive. But when a good hand turns sour on him, his pitch will invariably go up and his tone gets a rasping quality that is pretty irritating. This sign of his deteriorating hand usually comes a round or two before he stops betting or drops out. If his hand picks up again, his voice returns to normal.

Larry, an occasional player, always mumbles when he's confused about the value of his hand. At these times you'll hear such comments around the table as, "Did you call, Larry?" or "Did you say you're raising, Larry? How much?" When Larry's confident, on the other hand, he speaks up loudly and clearly.

Do any of the players in your group stutter, mispronounce words, or mix up words in a sentence? Do they do this all the time or only under stress? See how many voice changes you can pick up, and how accurately you can match them with the cards.

Idle Fingers

Whether you play with chips or cash, either one provides a toy for idle fingers to play with. Some players like to stack their chips or arrange their cash neatly on the table. Others heap it in front of them. Sometimes a player will finger a chip or coin unconsciously while he's thinking about betting. A player may pick up the chip or bill he's going to bet before it's his turn, signaling aggressively that he's got a good hand. This type of signal is usually deliberate and may even be outlawed in some groups.

It's the unconscious, occasional fingering that we're looking for. Do you notice a player sorting or counting the money in the pot only on rounds when he thinks he's going to win? Does another player fondle a chip whenever he's in deep thought or worried about his hand? Or does a player who normally plays with his chips stop when he gets an especially good, or tough hand to play?

George likes to keep his chips stacked neatly on the table. Normally he won't touch them during a hand except when betting. But on occasion, when he has a high stack in front of him, he'll knock it over upon receipt of an exceptional card.

When Mike has a small stack of chips in front of him and thinks he's working on a real winner, he's likely to eye his stack carefully, sometimes touching the chips, as if he's figuring out whether this stack will be enough for him to bet. I can usually tell when he's going to be betting light by this habit of his.

Facial Movements

Facial movements can be anything from an obvious yawn, grin, or grimace to light twitches, raised eyebrows, closing eyes, and puckering lips. While we've all heard of the "poker face," and some players come close to pulling it off, it's practically impossible to control every movement of our facial muscles.

The simple state of tiredness or boredom will tend to droop the eyelids. It would take exceptional control to keep those same droopy eyes while being dealt a pat four of a kind. Mike has two poker faces he uses on and off. Some nights he uses the comic side—always grinning, laughing, acting up, no matter what cards he has. Other times he puts on the tragic—serious, a little angry-looking. On a tragic night you can count on him to stay that way no matter how good a hand he gets. What he doesn't realize, however, is that he usually blinks more often when he's bluffing. This difference is slight, and I can't always predict accurately, but I've been able to often enough to make it worthwhile.

At your next game, study the faces of one or two particular players. Start with the easier ones and work on the poker faces later. See if you can detect any changes, however slight, that give away their hands. Look especially at the eyes and mouth.

Nervous Habits

Some players have nervous habits that become more pronounced during certain situations. If they have a facial tic or nervous laughter, does it get worse when their hands improve? Or does it disappear? Does a player tap his fingers when he's waiting anxiously for his turn to bet? Does another one grind his teeth when he's dealt a bad hand?

George has a nervous laugh that irritates everyone at the game. He says, "Heh, heh, heh," after practically every sentence. So I decided to study him to see if I could connect any changes in this nervous laugh of his to his luck in the game. I observed when the laughing increased or decreased and tried to match those times with the strength or weakness of his hand.

Since George wasn't a regular player, it took me a few months to get enough information. My conclusion? That his laugh had nothing to do with his game. But while observing him I noticed that he picked at his cuticles whenever he was in a tight situation.

Does anybody in your group display a nervous habit or mannerism that might give you a clue?

Attention

We give whatever we're doing various degrees of our attention. We may watch television and read a newspaper at the same time. If something interesting passes across the screen, we give it more attention, forgetting the newspaper. If a particular story in the paper draws our interest, we start reading word for word instead of idly scanning. If you observe the audience at a sports function, you'll see their excitement rise and ebb with the action on the field.

The same thing happens in poker. If you're sitting with a mediocre hand and the betting isn't very active, your attention won't be as great as when there's big money in the pot and your decision about what to replace could mean winning or losing it.

So, what kind of *attention* is each player showing in general, and specifically, to each of his cards? Does he suddenly perk up when he's dealt the K♥? Is he watching alertly every card that's dealt to the rest of the players, or is he staring fixedly at his own hand? Where is his attention focused on how intense is it?

Posture

Posture is sometimes part of attention and interest in the game. When a player is lounging back in his chair or slumped forward, he may be tired, bored, and disinterested in what's going on. Some players will sprawl out all over their chairs when they're feeling good. Others will sit up straight and lean over the table when they're having a winning streak.

Dave always takes a relaxed pose during the game. He makes a point of not showing too much interest in the game. Joey, however, starts out sitting in an active, aggressive, alert position. Then, as the game progresses, he has a few beers, and his interest in what's happening begins to wane, he falls back into a more relaxed slump. During that part of the evening he'll sit back up again only when he gets an especially promising hand.

George's shoulders often droop when he's not getting good cards. He seems to withdraw into a shell, protectively surrounding his cards and chips with his arms. At that point, Steve usually starts yelling that he can't see George's cards. That rings a bell somewhere inside George and he pops back up and bets aggressively for a round or two before giving up again and eventually dropping out.

Eating and Drinking

Is all the eating and drinking that goes on around the poker table strictly to satisfy hunger and thirst? Or for the fun of eating and drinking? What about the player who gets up for a cup of coffee after he's just lost a big pot? Or the player who celebrates winning a big hand by eating a sandwich?

More importantly, what about the player who obsessively eats pretzel after pretzel during a tense game, then relaxes after getting "his card" and stops eating? It's important to recognize which players use nibbling when they're concentrating hard, which ones do it when they're bored, and which ones do it when they expect to win the hand.

Sometimes a player who isn't having much luck will drink more heavily than usual. He's trying to forget the cards. Another player might do just the opposite—drink more when his luck is good and lay off it when things aren't going well.

Dave never eats anything during the game. And the only thing he'll drink is coffee. He's afraid to let anything interfere with his concentration. Every night he starts out with a cup of coffee. But I've been watching him to see if there's any pattern to his coffee drinking. I've noticed that his cup may sit on the table untouched for long periods. But when he's in a heavy game with high stakes, he tends to drink a few sips every couple of minutes throughout the hand. He doesn't stop this compulsive sipping until he's sure he's got the competition beat.

Joey is easily sidetracked with food. Put a bowl of anything edible in front of him, and that's where he concentrates his attention. So whenever I want to get his attention off the game, I pass him the pretzels.

Smoking

We had cigar, cigarette, and pipe smokers at our table. Also a couple of nonsmokers. Among the smokers, I tried to notice when they lit up, how long the intervals were between smokes, what made them forget the lit butt in the ashtray, and so on. Sometimes a guy will be concentrating on the game so hard with a cigarette in his hand that the ashes fall on the table. Even the way a person blows the smoke out of his mouth or nose may tell you something, if you can find the patterns.

One of the few telltale signs I've been able to catch Tom in is his cigar-smoking habits. I've noticed a slight tendency to keep the cigar in his mouth when he's confident, and to put it in the ashtray when he's concentrating on a tough game. When he's puffing away, he's generally in control, but when he's got a risky decision to make, he puts the cigar down and leaves it there until the crisis is over.

Doug is a nonsmoker. Invariably on bad nights he'll start complaining about the smoke in the room. If his bad luck continues, he'll get up and start opening windows, no matter what the weather is outside.

Mike is another nonsmoker. When he's not getting the cards he wants, he makes the smokers sitting next to him move their ashtrays to the other side. When luck is with him, he couldn't care less.

Emotion

The presence of strong emotions may change a player's normal mode of playing. When very angry, some people will play tighter, others looser. Some will play worse when they're embarrassed. Others will do so after they've been flattered.

Watch carefully to see what emotions are expressed during a game, and what effect these emotions have on the players. If a guy feels foolish after making a dumb move, does this affect his playing immediately afterward? If the group praises a player for an especially brilliant play, how does he take it? Does it make him try to live up to the reputation, or does it make him careless?

Sometimes an argument will arise in our game where one player will be accused of having done something wrong, for example, not splitting the pot correctly in hi-low, not putting his lights in at the end of the game, kibitzing during the game in a way that hurts another player, and so on. Some players can take it and play normally afterward. Others let their emotion get the best of them. For example, when Paul is angry he'll play very tight for the next four or five hands. And he's unable to pull off a bluff in this state of mind.

It's easy to tell when the outspoken players are feeling a strong emotion. They let you know verbally or by facial expression. But the poker faces may also be affected by emotions. The next time you see one of them insulted, or raise their voice even slightly in anger, watch their playing immediately after. Can you detect any change? The fact that they didn't express the emotion outwardly doesn't mean it wasn't affecting their play. Observe the emotional reactions of all players carefully.

Let's look at a sample hand to see how reading players can help you in a game:

Seven-Card Stud, Hi-Low

(bets are $1, $2, and $5 at any time, three raises maximum)

	George	Dave	Steve	Mike	Joey	Me
Card 1	////	////	////	////	////	A♥
Card 2	////	////	////	////	////	10♥♥
Card 3	A♣	A♣	10♣♣	J♥	7♦♦	3♦
	*bet $2	call	raise $5	call	call	call
	call	call				

In the first round of betting, George and Dave are sitting pretty with aces. George bets $2. Dave calls and Steve raises $5. This raise is typical for Steve. The rest of us call. I see George, Dave, Joey, and myself as potential lows at this point.

	George	Dave	Steve	Mike	Joey	Me
Card 1	////	////	////	////	////	A♥
Card 2	////	////	////	////	////	10♥♥
Card 3	A♣	A♣	10♣♣	J♥	7♦♦	3♦
	*bet $2	call	raise $5	call	call	call
	call	call				
Card 4	K♥	4♥ ♥	6♥ ♥	Q♥	6♠ ♠	2♠ ♠
	*bet $5	raise $5	call	call	call	call
	call					

The second up card eliminates George from the low group, especially when he knocks over his chips as he goes to bet $5. He's excited about that king, so I figure he must be going for high. Dave is a strong contender for low, especially when he raises $5. I figure he's trying to get me to drop or else has such a perfect first four cards that he's sure he's going to win half the pot. We all call around.

	George	Dave	Steve	Mike	Joey	Me
Card 1	▨	▨	▨	▨	▨	A♥
Card 2	▨	▨	▨	▨	▨	10♥
Card 3	A♣	A♦	10♣	J♥	7♦	3♦
	*bet $2	call	raise $5	call	call	call
	call	call				
Card 4	K♦	4♥	6♥	9♥	6♠	2♠
	*bet $5	raise $5	call	call	call	call
	call					
Card 5	7♣	8♠	10♦	2♥	5♣	6♦
			*check	bet $5	raise $5	raise $5
	call	call	raise $1	call	call	call
	call	call				

When the third up card is dealt, I show the strongest three cards for a low, Joey next with 5–6–7, and Dave next with 8–4–A. Steve shows a pair of 10s, but it doesn't seem to be helping him. He checks. Mike, showing three hearts, bets $5. We all figure he's going for a heart flush. Joey raises $5. Why not with three low cards and a possible straight showing? I raise and pass the potato chips to Joey. Since we may both be fighting for low, may as well distract him as much as possible. George calls. Dave calls, and I notice he's started sipping his coffee, indicating he's a little worried, obviously by what Joey and I are showing. Steve's voice gets high and raspy as he raises $1 to finish off the last raise. His hand seems to be busting. We all call around.

	George	Dave	Steve	Mike	Joey	Me
Card 1	▨	▨	▨	▨	▨	A♥
Card 2	▨	▨	▨	▨	▨	10♥♥♥
Card 3	A♣	A♣	10♣♣♣	J♥	7♦♦	3♦
	*bet $2	call	raise $5	call	call	call
	call	call				
Card 4	K♦	4♥♥	6♥♥	Q♥	6♠♠	2♠
	*bet $5	raise $5	call	call	call	call
	call					
Card 5	7♣♣	8♠♠	10♦♦	2♥	5♣♣	6♦♦
			*check	bet $5	raise $5	raise $5
	call	call	raise $1	call	call	call
	call	call				
Card 6	4♠♠	3♣	2♣	3♠	9♠♠	5♦♦
			*check	bet $5	raise $5	raise $5
	call	raise $1	call	call	call	call
	call					

After the last up card is dealt, George's hand shows three low cards, but his shoulders are drooping. Evidently it was the high he was going after originally and it's not working out. Dave is still sipping coffee, in spite of his A–4–8–3 showing. He's obviously worried about my 3–2–6–5 showing. I figure Dave at this point probably has at best an 8 or 7 low. Joey's low didn't improve with the 9, although he may already have a 7–6 low. He could also be going for the straight. Steve's hand shows a pair of 10s and two clubs—hard to tell what he has. Mike shows three hearts and a spade, probably going for the heart flush.

Steve opens with a check, but his voice is back to normal. Mike bets $5. Joey raises $5, I raise $5. George calls. Dave raises $1, still sipping coffee, proving me right about him. Steve calls. That last card seemed to have helped him. I figure maybe he's going for a club flush. We call around.

	George	Dave	Steve	Mike	Joey	Me
Card 1	(hidden)	(hidden)	(hidden)	(hidden)	(hidden)	A♥
Card 2	(hidden)	(hidden)	(hidden)	(hidden)	(hidden)	10♥
Card 3	A♣	A♠	10♣	J♥	7♦	3♦
	*bet $2	call	raise $5	call	call	call
	call	call				
Card 4	K♥	4♥	6♥	Q♥	6♠	2♠
	*bet $5	raise $5	call	call	call	call
	call					
Card 5	7♣	8♠	10♦	2♥	5♣	6♦
			*check	bet $5	raise $5	raise $5
	call	call	raise $1	call	call	call
	call	call				
Card 6	4♠	3♣	2♣	3♠	9♠	5♦
			*check	bet $5	raise $5	raise $5
	call	raise $1	call	call	call	call
	call					
Card 7	(hidden)	(hidden)	(hidden)	(hidden)	(hidden)	9♥
			*check	bet $5	call	raise $5
	raise $5	raise $1	call	call	call	call
	call					

After the last card is dealt, Steve checks again. Mike bets $5, but I notice he's blinking a lot—probably didn't catch the heart flush after all. Joey is working on the potato chips as he calls the bet. I raise $5. George is humped over with his arms around his cards. Steve yells at him and he sits up suddenly and raises $5. Dave raises $1. We all call around.

	George	Dave	Steve	Mike	Joey	Me
Card 1	(hidden)	(hidden)	(hidden)	(hidden)	(hidden)	A♡
Card 2	(hidden)	(hidden)	(hidden)	(hidden)	(hidden)	10♡♡♡
Card 3	A♣	A♠	10♣♣♣	J♡	7♦♦	3♦
	*bet $2	call	raise $5	call	call	call
	call	call				
Card 4	K♦	4♡ ♡	6♡ ♡	Q♡	6♠ ♠	2♠
	*bet $5	raise $5	call	call	call	call
	call					
Card 5	7♣ ♣	8♠ ♠	10♦♦♦	2♡	5♣ ♣	6♦ ♦
			*check	bet $5	raise $5	raise $5
	call	call	raise $1	call	call	call
	call	call				
Card 6	4♠ ♠	3 ♣	2 ♣	3 ♠	9♠ ♠	5♦ ♦
			*check	bet $5	raise $5	raise $5
	call	raise $1	call	call	call	call
	call					
Card 7	(hidden)	(hidden)	(hidden)	(hidden)	(hidden)	9♡ ♡
			*check	bet $5	call	raise $5
	raise $5	raise $1	call	call	call	call
	call					
	HIGH	LOW	HIGH	HIGH	LOW	LOW
			*check	bet $5	raise $1	raise $5
	fold	raise $1	call	call	call	call

George, Steve, and Mike declare high. Dave, Joey, and I declare low. Steve checks. Mike bets $5, still blinking. Joey raises $1. I figure he's in for the duration with a 7–6 low. If Joey had a 6–5 low he'd be raising $5 not $1. I raise $5. George folds. Dave takes the last raise for $1. Everyone else calls.

	George	Dave	Steve	Mike	Joey	Me
Card 1	K♠	7♥	8♣	9♦	2♦	A♥
Card 2	A♦	5♠	9♣	J♦	4♣	10♥
Card 3	A♣	A♠	10♣	J♥	7♦	3♦
Card 4	K♦	4♥	6♥	Q♥	6♠	2♠
Card 5	7♣	8♠	10♦	2♥	5♣	6♦
Card 6	4♠	3♣	2♣	3♠	9♠	5♦
Card 7	10♠	Q♦	Q♣	5♥	K♣	9♥
	HIGH	LOW	HIGH	HIGH	LOW	LOW
			Winner			*Winner*

Steve wins high with a club flush. I win low with a 6–5–3–2–A. Mike was bluffing. Joey had the 7–6 low, and Dave had a 7–5 low.

Betting Patterns

MOST PLAYERS DEVELOP a fairly regular betting pattern, or style. While they may bet or raise for various reasons—to build the pot, to bluff, to get another player out—they tend to form habitual ways of doing this. For example, one player may normally bet the maximum when dealt two pair in five-card draw. Another player may check with this hand. Some dealers of five-card draw will always open, no matter what they hold, if the hand has been checked around to them.

If you can figure out the betting patterns of the players in your group, you'll have a better idea of what a check, bet, or raise means. While you may not always be able to tell the exact implications, by putting this information together with all the rest of your data you'll be able to make more accurate predictions.

The first step again is observation. Make a mental note of a player's betting during a game. Then check it against his hand at the end of the play. Did he have his strength initially? When did his betting get heavier? What kind of competition did he see in the hands around him? When you fold a hand, use that opportunity to study what the others are doing. If there are players who don't mind your looking over their shoulder, this is an excellent way to get information about the way they play.

Opening

What makes a player open? In draw, does he bet strictly on his own hand, or does position count? If he was going to open, but a player before him bets out, does he then simply call, or does he raise? If he's the dealer, or next to last to bet, or the first to bet, how does this position affect his betting?

In stud, some players always open with a bet if they're high on the board. In five-card stud, high only, practically anyone will bet the maximum in limit poker if they're high on board, although some players will only do so if they show a king or ace. The players in my group always opened with $5 if they were high on board in five-card stud, unless their card was lower than a jack and they had a low card in the hole.

In hi-low five-card stud, some players will open if they show the lowest card on board. Others will require a low card in the hole also to do this. And other players won't open on the low at all. They'll call the high bettor, but they won't open if it's checked around. This is because it's so easy to bust a low in five-card stud. The player who opens reasons that he's got the best low hand at the moment and his bet might get the other potential lows out of the game.

In six- and seven-card stud games, most players want at least two good cards in order to open on the first round. If they're going high, they'll want at least a high pair, or three to a straight or flush. A looser player may open with three high cards, or a low pair if he's high on board, or it's been checked around to him. A conservative player will want three good cards or a pair of aces before he opens. Going low, the loose player will open on two good cards, or with an ace showing. The conservative player will require three good cards unless he's the only one showing a low card. You'll find that some players have very specific requirements about when they'll open. For example, they may open with two cards under 6, but not with a 7, or they'll want an ace and another low card, or else three low cards.

Usually in a game with wild cards most players will upgrade their opening requirements. If it will take a better hand to win the game, they need better cards to start with. The same thing goes for games in which you get many cards, such as Anaconda. Here, you'll need at least a high full house in order to win high and probably a 6–4 to win low. Many times Anaconda will be checked the first round of betting, since three cards have to be passed and even a good hand can be ruined by that first pass.

In games with a widow, some players will open on the basis of a good potential hand. Others want to see what's in the widow first, unless the cards they hold are solid. For example, one player might open with four low cards in his hand, hoping to find the fifth in the widow. Another player with the same hand might prefer to check and wait.

If you play the same games fairly regularly, it's easier to figure out the betting patterns. You'll have more opportunity to study the players in a particular game. Also, when playing the same game, a player will tend to form habits. If the games are many and varied, a player will have less chance to develop a standard play.

Raising

Just as certain opening habits are developed by most players, so are raising habits. There are two basic reasons for raising a bet: to build the pot that you expect to split, and to chase another player out in order to increase your chances of splitting the pot. Some players will also raise a low bet simply because it's uninteresting to play poker for a small pot.

You must find out how strong a player's hand must be before he'll raise. At one end of the scale we have the most conservative, tight player who will only raise when he has all his cards, that is, five cards for a flush, low or straight, four of a kind, a full house, and so on. This kind of player also requires that no other player indicates a better hand either by the cards that are showing or the betting. Such a purely tight player probably doesn't exist in actuality. If he did, reading him would be easy and every one would know to fold as soon as he began to raise.

On the other end of the scale is the extreme loose player, who will raise on a hope and a prayer. He'll raise holding only one or two good cards, with the expectation that his hands will fill in later. Most players fall somewhere in the middle of these two extremes. They take into consideration the cards they hold now, their chances of filling in, and the relative strength of this hand in relation to what they see in the other players' hands.

However, there are variations. Some players will raise "on the come" more than others. The trick is to figure out just where on the scale each player stands.

Further complicating this is the raising done in order to chase out another player. This is why a player may raise one round and not the next, even though his hand may have stayed the same or improved. He tried it once to see whom he could scare out. He knows it won't work again. Of course, if he does scare his opponents out, he may raise the next time because he now expects to win.

Sometimes two or three players will get together to force another player out. They're not exactly collaborating, but merely relying on the knowledge that the next guy will raise also. This depends on position. For example, if A wants to get E out, and he knows that B and C are going to raise, A will bet or raise (when he ordinarily would check or call) because he figures the cumulative effect of three raises will be too much for E.

So you've got to be able to sort out the raising to chase out and the raising on the basis of a solid hand. By observing players you'll notice some of them hardly ever raise to chase out, while others do it constantly. By using this information, you'll be able to get a more accurate picture of the betting patterns.

There's also the opposite of raising to get other players out: not raising in order to keep other players in. This is done by a player who has a strong hand, expects to win the pot, but doesn't want to scare everyone out. He has to determine whether raising and possibly dropping a few players will bring in a bigger pot than calling and having everybody stay in. Often, a player with a good hand will sit back and call when one or more other players are raising. The raising is done for him, so the pot is being built without his having to give away his strong hand. Keep your eyes open for this by observing other signs of the strength of a player's hand mentioned throughout this book.

Steve is a fairly easy player to read in the beginning of a game. He'll open early on mediocre to good cards, and raise to chase out other players. George, on the other hand, is usually conservative early in the game. He'll open only if his cards are very good, and he doesn't raise to chase very often. When he raises, it's on the basis of his own good hand. Dave has the knack of knowing when his raising won't force other players to fold. This enables him to get a lot of mileage out of his good hands. This works especially well for him in hi-low games, where he counts on two or three players going for the other half of the pot to stay in for his raises.

Changes in Betting Patterns

Although you may be able to pigeonhole a player in a particular betting pattern, there are times when his pattern will change. For example, a player who never opened on seven-card stud without a pair of aces or better may start opening on a pair of 9s. A player who normally raises on the hopes of filling in his last two cards may only call on such a hand. A player who never raises to chase another out may begin to do so.

What causes these changes in betting patterns, and how can you detect them? To answer the second part of the question first, you've simply got to be constantly aware and alert. Once you label a player, don't forget him. You may be counting on that label some day when it's no longer descriptive. So when you see a player do something odd or different, check it out. Is he playing according to his usual style, or has he changed?

What makes a player change? A long losing streak or even a short losing streak may account for it, although some players never seem to be able to change their betting patterns. It's the player who says to himself, "Hey, I must be doing something wrong. Maybe I'm betting too much." Or, "Maybe I'm not betting enough." He makes a conscious effort to change his betting pattern, hoping that that will improve his game.

Sometimes a player will read a book or get some advice from another poker player. If they've been opening on a pair of deuces and the book says they must have a pair of kings or better, they'll tighten up their play. Dave likes to give other players advice, and our group even developed nicknames for types of players, such as "Crowbar," for someone who can't be chased out of the game. Joey was the one most often called "Crowbar," although other players earned the title occasionally. For example, when Dave got to Joey, he was likely to change his betting patterns temporarily.

Sometimes a player changes his betting pattern according to his mood. When he's feeling well and lucky, he'll open and raise more readily than when he's feeling low and unlucky. Personal problems, alertness, alcohol intake—all can have an influence on a player's betting patterns. This is why you have to observe each player under various conditions to see how and why his patterns change.

Staying and Minimizing the Bet

There are players who rarely raise, but will always call someone else's bet unless they have pure garbage. Other players will either be aggressively betting and raising, or they will fold. Some people like to be leaders, others feel more comfortable being followers.

In general, a player will have a rough guideline he's set up for himself that tells him when he should open, when he should raise, when he should call, and when he should fold. In addition to the relative value of his hand, he takes into consideration the size of the pot, the size of the bet, and how much it will cost him to see the next card, or stay in until the end.

Some players, conservative in their raising habits, do so only with exceptionally good chances or winning; nonetheless they tend to be loose in their staying habits. Sometimes they'll take a raise for the lowest amount in order to minimize a bet. This can only happen when the betting amounts and number of raises are specified, or limited, of course. For example, if three raises are allowed and the betting amounts are $1, $2, or $5, a player who wants to stay for the minimum amount of money possible may take a raise for $1 in order to keep other players from making $5 raises. If a player misses an opportunity to do this, when it's obvious he can and should, you may wonder whether he's doing it from lack of judgment or if he's hiding a much better hand than he admits to.

Some players will base their staying in large part on how much money they've already put in the pot. Given the same hand and cards showing around the board, a player might drop out if he had little money in the pot, but stay in if he'd already invested a sizable amount. Of course, this is also related to the size of the pot and how much he stands to win if he stays. This is so because, if a player has stayed in for raises early in the game, he's more likely to stay in on raises later on. If the betting has been light early in the game, there's not as much cause for a player with a marginal hand to stay in later on.

Sometimes a player who begins to bet out early in the game, with a high potential hand, will find that the subsequent cards bust his hand. While one player may drop immediately when this happens, another may continue to bet, or at least call, for another round or two. The momentum of his early betting keeps him going. Sometimes, a player will even be embarrassed to show that his hand has deteriorated so rapidly. He feels he's revealing poor judgment if he was betting heavily early and then drops out, so he stays in for a while longer. He may even decide to bluff at this stage. Mike will often switch from raising because of a good hand to raising in order to bluff. George, on the other hand, will tend to simply stay after his good hand has started to deteriorate. Eventually he folds. Once in a while he'll move into the bluff stage and continue betting heavily, but his situation is often obvious.

Conservative Players

The conservative player usually doesn't lose much money. But he doesn't win much either. He may do well in some circles, but he becomes less effective as the other players get on to his style and learn to use the information to their own advantage.

In general, the conservative player won't take chances. He requires better cards to open, to raise, and to call than the average player does. He doesn't go after the long shots, and isn't a gambler. He doesn't mind not playing many hands, and has no insatiable desire to "see the next card." He's pretty self-controlled and bluffs just often enough to let the other players know he's capable of doing it. He generally relies more on his own cards than on his predictions about other players' hands. If his cards meet a certain standard he's set for himself, he's likely to stay in, unless presented with strong evidence that he's beaten by another player. Dave is the conservative player in our group. He started out winning quite a bit, but gradually, as the rest of us learned to deal with his style, he won less and less. In addition, he found it tough to deal with Tom, who is a good player, but not a conservative one, and difficult to read.

System Players

A system player is conservative in the sense that he follows a particular system. When you don't know what the system is, however, his play can appear quite erratic. Obviously, then, the more complex the system, the more difficult it's going to be for you to pin down what's happening.

Once again, you've got to look for patterns. Try for the simple explanation. There's a system in five-card stud, for example, that says your first two cards must add up to nineteen in order to stay in (aces count eleven, picture cards ten, others face value). A player who rigidly follows this system would be easy to read, once you were on to him. If his up card is an 8 you know he's got to have an ace or an 8 in the hole if he stays in or bets.

Since most systems are developed to assure the system player a winning hand in the long run, you can use your general reading techniques even if you don't know what the system is. Looking again at the five-card stud system, for example, even if you didn't know about the nineteen rule, you'd at least figure out that the guy would only stay in or bet with two quite high cards. So rather than trying to figure out the precise system a player uses, look for overall patterns.

If you are a system player, you can use the material in this book to increase your system's effectiveness. For example, if you use the nineteen rule in five-card stud, there are times when it would pay you to override your system. Let's stay, for example, that you are dealt a 9 and a 10. Your system says to stay in. But the opener makes a high bet and another player raises. You know that these two are conservative players, and one especially would never raise without a high pair. With this information, you can save yourself some money by dropping out, in spite of your system. In other words, you'd use your system as a general guide, but modify it according to the information you process about other players' hands.

Actors and Reactors

The extremely active player makes his decisions based solely on his own hand, regardless of what other players show. The extreme reactive player makes his decision solely on what he thinks the other players have. Obviously, one couldn't play poker very well at either extreme. One has to consider one's own hand, but unless you've got a royal flush or a perfect low, you also have to consider its worth relative to the hands around you. While no player is totally actor or totally reactor, they do tend to fall more to one side or the other.

The player who uses a system or sets up standards for his hand is usually more of an actor. If he's figured that a 7–5 low has a good chance of winning in seven-card stud hi-low, he'll probably stay in with a 7–5 or better low hand. If he's convinced a flush has a good chance of winning a particular game, and he has four cards to a flush with three chances left and few of his suit showing, he'll probably stay in. While he does look around, and will drop out if he's obviously beaten by another player, he still bases his decisions more on his own cards than on what he reads in the other hands.

The reactive player, on the other hand, will always judge his hand's *relative* value, not its absolute value. In one game he may stay in with a pair of 5s, while in another of the same game he may drop with a straight. He spends most of his energy trying to figure out what the other players have, and bases his decision more on how he thinks his hand stacks up against them.

The active player counts on the card probabilities. If the probabilities tell him that his hand is likely to win, he'll stay in, even with evidence that another player has gotten a long shot and beaten him. In a game where one player makes a hand with one-in-fifty odds, the active players will probably be in at the end of the hand, because they were counting on the probabilities to keep that one player from getting it. The reactive player, however, will have read the other signs and dropped out.

When you come right down to it, reactive skills are the ones that produce big winners. If you can learn to judge accurately what's happening in your opponents' hands, it will be a simple matter to judge whether or not yours will beat them. It's the reactive skills that we're concentrating on in this book.

The reason I bring the point up in this chapter is that you need to know in which category a player falls in order to judge his betting accurately. If he's an active player, his betting patterns will be based more on the cards he has in his own hand. If he's a reactive player, his betting decisions will be based more on what he sees in the hands around him. By figuring out which type of player you're dealing with, you'll know whether to look at his cards or to put yourself in his position observing the other players' cards.

Tom was the biggest winner in our game because he's a reactive player, and a good one. He always made his decisions based on the *relative* value of his hand, and he was a good reader, so his decisions were often correct. I've seen him fold a hand that another player would be loath to let go. And I've seen him stay on a hand that the probabilities would say was a pretty certain loser.

Steve switches back and forth. Sometimes he'll play very actively, ignoring obvious signs. Other times he'll overreact to what he sees on the board and drop when he should have stayed. That's the general problem with reactive playing. It only works if you're good at it. If your judgment of the other players is poor, you'll lose more money than a conservative active player would. So don't give up active playing until you perfect your reactive skills.

Position

Position also affects betting patterns. In some games such as draw poker, position is very important on the opening bet. The dealer has an advantage, since he's the last bettor. A mediocre hand that wouldn't ordinarily be opened on may prove to be a winner if everyone checks to him. By hearing all the other players bet first, he gets more information than any other player about the strength of everyone's hand.

Whom you sit next to on the left- or right-hand side is also important. If you sit to the left of a player who typically raises, such as Steve, you'll be able to let him do the raising for you if you've got a good hand, and be able to drop out if you've got a poor hand. If you were on his right and had to bet first, you wouldn't know whether he was going to raise that time or not. If you call the bet on a mediocre hand, Steve might raise and then it would cost you more money to stay in, or you'd drop and lose the money you already put in. You won't know whether to count on him to raise if you've got a good hand.

Position is also important when you're betting to chase someone out. If the person you're trying to chase out is sitting immediately to your left, he'll have less information to go on to make his choice if you raise. He'd like to know what the other players are going to do first, but he doesn't. So you have an advantage.

Position will also affect opportunities to minimize the bet. If you have seven players in a game, and the strong players follow each other in the betting, they're likely to take all the raises for maximum amounts. On the other hand, the weaker players could make minimum raises and keep the total bet down.

When we declared high or low at the end of a game, we all did it together by putting zero, one, or two chips in our fist and then opening our hands at the same time. In some games, however, the declaration is made one at a time, in order. It may be done from the dealer's left, or from the last bettor or raiser. In this case, position would be very important. Obviously, if everyone else has declared high and you're the last declarer, you're assured of half the hand if you declare low.

In games where cards can be replaced, position is again important. Seeing who replaces high cards and who replaces low cards in a hi-low game, for example, helps you decide what your chances are for going either way. We had a game called Six Stud with Replace in which each player is dealt two cards down, then four cards up, and then may replace either two cards or none. It's a high-low game. The player with the highest hand on board is the first to remove the two cards he wants to replace. But rather than give each person his cards at that time, we went all the way around first. After everyone had discarded two or no cards, we then replaced the discarded cards. While this offers some information to players in the last positions, it doesn't offer as much as if the cards were replaced as they were discarded.

Be sure you know what the replacement rules are in the group you play with. If there's a lot of position advantage, you have to take that into consideration when making your playing decisions. In games where the last bettor or raiser gets the first, or worst, position, this fact will affect the betting. If a player doesn't want this position, he's likely not to bet or raise.

You have to be aware of position not only from your own point of view, but how it affects the betting habits of the other players. You should be aware, for example, when a player is avoiding betting because he hasn't got the cards and when he's doing it because of the position he's in. If the first bettor opens in draw poker, for example, it may have a different value than if everyone were to check and the dealer opened.

Some dealers of draw poker will always open if everyone else has checked. Some players will hesitate to open on a fairly strong hand if they are immediately to the left of the dealer. So study the effects of position in the various games your group plays, and how these positions affect each player's normal betting habits.

Let's look at a game of Six Stud with Replace now to see how knowledge of betting patterns can help decision-making:

Six Stud With Replace

(Played like six-card stud, except that, starting from high hand on board, players may replace two cards or none. Betting is $1, $2, and $5, three raises maximum. Cost of replacing the two cards is $5. High and low hands split the pot.)

	Tom	Steve	Me	Mike	George	Dave
Card 1	/////	/////	9♠ ♠	/////	/////	/////
Card 2	/////	/////	7♦ ♦	/////	/////	/////
Card 3	A♣	6♦ ♦	5♦ ♦	5♠ ♠	2 ♡	4♡ ♡
	*bet $5	call	call	call	raise $5	raise $5
	call	call	call	call	call	

In the first round, Tom bets $5 on his ace. Everyone is showing one very good low card. We all call until George, who raises $5. I figure he must have three good low cards. When Dave raises $5 I wonder what his motive is. I doubt he'd raise on three good cards for a low with all the low hands indicated, especially after George showed a strong enough hand to raise on.

	Tom	Steve	Me	Mike	George	Dave
Card 1	/////	/////	9♠ ♠	/////	/////	/////
Card 2	/////	/////	7♦ ♦	/////	/////	/////
Card 3	A♣	6♦ ♦	5♦ ♦	5♠ ♠	2 ♡	4♡ ♡
	*bet $5	call	call	call	raise $5	raise $5
	call	call	call	call	call	
Card 4	8♣ ♣	3 ♡	2 ♦	2 ♠	8♠ ♠	Q♠
	*check	bet $5	call	raise $5	call	raise $5
	raise $1	call	call	call	call	call

In the next round, Tom checks his 8♣. Steve, who now has two low cards showing, bets $5. I call. Mike, who also shows two low cards, raises $5. George calls. The 8 didn't help him much. Dave raises $5 again, after getting the Q♠, which makes me think he's possibly going high, but I'm not sure with what. Tom takes the last raise for $1 to minimize the bet, and we all call. I

71

stay in on the basis of the three diamonds, the possible straight, and the 2–5–7 to a low.

	Tom	Steve	Me	Mike	George	Dave
Card 1	▨	▨	9♠	▨	▨	▨
Card 2	▨	▨	7♦	▨	▨	▨
Card 3	A♣	6♦	5♦	5♠	2♥	4♥
	*bet $5	call	call	call	raise $5	raise $5
	call	call	call	call	call	
Card 4	8♣	3♥	2♦	2♠	8♠	Q♠
	*check	bet $5	call	raise $5	call	raise $5
	raise $1	call	call	call	call	call
Card 5	10♥	A♥	8♦	5♣	J♦	Q♥
						*bet $5
	fold	raise $5	fold	raise $1	call	raise $5
		call		call	call	

In the next round, Dave's $5 bet after getting another queen confirms that he's going for high, probably with a full house or even four of a kind. There are no 4s or queens showing on the board in anyone else's hand. Tom folds. His weak betting on the previous card, the 8, and his fold now after getting the 10 indicate to me he was going low but is convinced there are better lows on the board. I also figure, if he had been going for high, Dave's showing and strong betting (for such a conservative player) means there's no hope there. Steve, who now shows three beautiful low cards, raises $5. I fold my hand, even though it shows possibilities for a diamond flush, a straight, and 8–7–5–2 toward a low. Steve, Mike, and George are all obviously going for low, and Dave in all likelihood has the winning high hand that would beat a straight or a flush.

Mike raises $1 to minimize the bet. Pairing up on 5s hasn't helped his low. George, who has stopped raising since the first round, is nevertheless calling. If it was another player calling you might suspect them of having a better hand than they let on since he didn't take the $1 minimum raise. But with George you can be pretty sure he just forgot about it. As predicted, Dave takes the last raise for $5 and everyone calls around.

	Tom	Steve	Me	Mike	George	Dave
Card 1			9♠			
Card 2			7♦			
Card 3	A♣	6♦	5♦	5♠	2♥	4♥
	*bet $5	call	call	call	raise $5	raise $5
	call	call	call	call	call	
Card 4	8♣	3♥	2♦	2♠	8♠	Q♠
	*check	bet $5	call	raise $5	call	raise $5
	raise $1	call	call	call	call	call
Card 5	10♥	A♥	8♦	5♣	J♦	Q♥
						*bet $5
	fold	raise $5	fold	raise $1	call	raise $5
		call		call	call	call
Card 6		J♣		J♥	10♦	K♠
						*bet $5
		call		call	call	

The last card shows no improvement for anyone. Dave bets $5 again and he's called around. Since Dave is high on board, he will have to replace first. He is staying pat, confirming my suspicion of a full house or four of a kind, although with four of a kind some players would replace two to try to fool someone. Dave wouldn't want to waste the $5 it costs to replace.

Steve asks for one down and one up card. His replaced up card is the J♣. Mike, also going low, replaces the 5♣ and J♥. George replaces the J♦ and 10♦. All three are going low. Steve gets his replacement cards first: one card down and the 6♥ up. He's paired up his 6s, but we don't know what the down card was. Mike gets a Q♣ and 10♣, no help. George gets a K♥ and 3♠. The best he can have is an 8 low with two good down cards.

	Tom	Steve	Me	Mike	George	Dave
Card 1	(hidden)	(hidden)	9♠	(hidden)	(hidden)	(hidden)
Card 2	(hidden)	(hidden)	7♦	(hidden)	(hidden)	(hidden)
Card 3	A♣	6♦	5♦	5♠	2♥	4♥
	*bet $5	call	call	call	raise $5	raise $5
	call	call	call	call	call	
Card 4	8♣	3♥	2♦	2♠	8♠	Q♠ (hidden)
	*check	bet $5	call	raise $5	call	raise $5
	raise $1	call	call	call	call	call
Card 5	10♥	A♥	8♦	5♣	J♦ (hidden)	Q♥ (hidden)
						*bet $5
	fold	raise $5	fold	raise $1	call	raise $5
		call		call	call	
Card 6		J♣ (hidden)		J♥ (hidden)	10♦	K♠ (hidden)
						*bet $5
		call		call	call	
		replaces		replaces	replaces	stays pat
		J♣ (hidden)		J♥ (hidden), 5♣	J♦ (hidden), 10♦	
		gets		gets	gets	
		6♥ (hidden)		Q♣ (hidden), 10♣	K♥ (hidden), 3♠	
						*bets $5
		raise $5		fold	raise $5	raise $5
		call			call	

Dave bets $5. Steve raises $5, either because he caught the right card or is bluffing. Mike has nothing even to bluff with, and folds. George raises $5. He obviously doesn't believe Steve got it. Dave raises $5. Steve and George call.

In the declaration, however, Steve surprises us. He goes high, with Dave. George goes low. Now I figure Steve might possibly have caught a heart flush and thinks Dave didn't replace cards because he wanted to present a strong front and only had two pair, or three of a kind. Whatever Steve was thinking, after

George bets $5 and Dave raises $5, Steve raises $1 to minimize
the bet. George takes the last raise for $5, it's called around, and
everyone shows their hands. Dave had the full house, 4s up.
George had the 8 low. Steve did catch a heart flush at the end.

Cards Held Before the Replace

	Tom	Steve	Me	Mike	George	Dave
Card 1	K♣	5♡	9♠	3♣	A♢	4♣
Card 2	2♣	K♢	7♢	7♠	6♠	4♠
Card 3	A♣	6♢	5♢	5♠	2♡	4♡
Card 4	8♣	3♡	2♢	2♠	8♠	Q♢
Card 5	10♡	A♡	8♢	5♣	J♢	Q♡
Card 6		J♣		J♡	10♢	K♠

Cards Held After the Replace

		Steve		Mike	George	Dave
Card 1		5♡		3♣	A♢	4♣
Card 2		9♡		7♠	6♠	4♠
Card 3		6♢		5♠	2♡	4♡
Card 4		3♡		2♠	8♠	Q♢
Card 5		A♡		Q♣	3♠	Q♡
Card 6		6♡		10♣	K♡	K♠
		HIGH			LOW	HIGH
					Winner	*Winner*

Betting Pace

THE AMOUNT OF MONEY on the table in table stakes, or the size of the bets in limit poker, will have a direct influence upon the amount of money available to be won in an evening of poker. The number of players and hours played are other obvious factors. But two groups of the same number of players may play for the same stakes for the same length of time with a big difference in the average pot size for the two groups. Why? Because of betting pace.

For example, take Group I with six players and Group II with six players, both groups playing for limits of $1, $2, and $5, with three raises the maximum. In Group I they play mostly high-only games of straight five- and seven-card stud and five-card draw. They play no push, replacement, or rollover games. The players are relaxed and sociable. They talk a lot during the game. They play with one deck of cards, and often there's a wait between hands while someone gets around to shuffling and figuring out whose deal it is. They take time out during the evening to eat sandwiches. The bets are mostly for $1 and $2 on the first cards. There are few raises.

Group II plays mostly hi-low games. They like pay-to-push games, replacements, and rollovers. They confine their talking pretty much to comments about the game, unless they're out. They use two decks of cards, keeping one ready all the time, with an efficient system for dealing and shuffling. If a player forgets his deal or shuffle, he's quickly reminded by one of the other players. If anyone wants to eat or drink, they take care of it while playing, or when they're out. The bets are rarely for $1 or $2, starting with $5 early in each game. There are many raises.

Will Group I or II have the highest pots and the largest amount of money bet during the evening? Group II will, obviously. The same quality playing will lose more in Group II or win more in Group II. Therefore, it offers the largest potential winnings for the good player. If you look at the winnings and losses of both groups over a period of time, the average biggest winner and biggest loser each night will have lost or won more money in Group II than in Group I. The only person who won't be affected is the guy whose playing falls right in the middle. If his winnings and losses always average out to zero, it won't matter which group he plays with.

What's the Betting Pace in Your Group?

Do players usually start out by making small bets? Are there many rounds where everyone checks? How good must the players' cards be for them to make large bets? Do their bets increase on the second round of betting? The third round? The fourth round? Do they bet the maximum only on the last card?

What about raising? Try keeping track of the actual number of raises that are made during a typical game the group plays regularly. Then keep track the next time it's played, and compare. Do this five or six times during an evening and see how consistent the playing is. Let's look at the following sample betting pattern for a game of seven-card stud:

Player:	A	B	C	D	E	F
Round 1			*bet	call	call	call
	call	call				
Round 2	*bet	call	raise	call	call	fold
	call	call				
Round 3	*bet	call	raise	fold	raise	
	call	call	call			
Round 4	*check	check	bet		call	
	raise	fold	raise		call	
	call					
Round 5	*bet		call		call	

*Indicates opener, on following sample betting patterns.

There were no raises in round 1, one raise in round 2, two raises in round 3, two raises in round 4, and no raises in round 5, making (0 + 1 + 2 + 2 + 0) five raises in all.

If you notice in a game of seven-card stud that there were eight raises throughout the game, check out the next game to see if this is a typical number. Suppose you end up with the following:

Game #:	1	2	3	4	5	6
Raises:	8	3	10	7	8	9

Altogether there were forty-five raises in six games, or 7.5 average raises per game.

A game of seven-card stud that has less than six raises produces a fairly slow betting pace. But you also have to take into consideration the size of the bets. How many bets (or raises) of minimum, median, and maximum bets are made during a typical hand? If all the bets and raises are of the minimum variety, the pot will remain small.

The next thing you have to consider is how many players stay in for the raises. Does everyone but the two or three with the best hands drop at the first raise? Or at the other extreme, do you often end up with six or seven players still in at the end of the hand? Let's look at some sample betting patterns and see how the size of the bet, the number of raises, and the dropping of players affect the pot. We'll assume limits of $1, $2, and $5 can be bet at any time, with a maximum of three raises.

Game 1

(bets are low, infrequent raises, many players fold)

Player:	A	B	C	D	E	F	G	Pot size
Round 1				*bet $1	call	fold	call	
	call	fold	call					$5
Round 2				*bet $1	call		call	
	raise $2		call	call	call		call	$20
Round 3			*bet $1	call	raise $1		fold	
	call		call	call				$28
Round 4			*bet $2	fold	raise $2			
	fold		call					$36
Round 5			*bet $1		raise $5			
			raise $5		call			$58

Game 2

(bets are low, infrequent raises, few players fold)

Player:	A	B	C	D	E	F	G	Pot size
Round 1				*bet $1	call	call	call	
	call	call	call					$7
Round 2				*bet $1	call	call	call	
	raise $2	call	call	call	call	call	call	$28
Round 3			*bet $1	call	raise $1	call	call	
	call	fold	call	call				$40
Round 4			*bet $2	call	raise $2	fold	call	
	call		call	call				$60
Round 5			*bet $1	fold	raise $5		call	
	call		raise $5		call		fold	
	call							$99

Game 3

(bets are low, frequent raises, many players fold)

Player:	A	B	C	D	E	F	G	Pot size
Round 1				*bet $1	raise $1	fold	call	
	raise $1	fold	call	call	call		call	$15
Round 2				*bet $1	call		call	
	raise $2		call	call	call		call	$30
Round 3			*bet $1	raise $1	raise $1		fold	
	raise $1		call	call	call			$46
Round 4			*bet $2	fold	raise $2			
	fold		raise $2		raise $2			
			call					$62
Round 5			*bet $1		raise $5			
			raise $5		raise $5			
			call					$94

Game 4

(bets are low, frequent raises, few players fold)

Player:	A	B	C	D	E	F	G	Pot size
Round 1				*bet $1	raise $1	call	call	
	raise $1	call	call	call	call	call	call	$21
Round 2				*bet $1	call	call	call	
	raise $2	call	call	call	call	call	call	$42
Round 3			*bet $1	raise $1	raise $1	call	call	
	raise $1	fold	call	call	call	call	call	$66
Round 4			*bet $2	call	raise $2	fold	call	
	call		raise $2	call	raise $2		call	
	call		call	call				$106
Round 5			*bet $1	fold	raise $5		call	
	call		raise $5		raise $5		fold	
	call		call					$160

Game 5

(bets are high, infrequent raises, many players fold)

Player:	A	B	C	D	E	F	G	Pot size
Round 1				*bet $5	call	fold	call	
	call	fold	call					$25
Round 2				*bet $5	call		call	
	raise $5		call	call	call		call	$75
Round 3			*bet $5	call	raise $5		fold	
	call		call	call				$115
Round 4			*bet $5	fold	raise $5			
	fold		call					$135
Round 5			*bet $5		raise $5			
			raise $5		call			$165

Game 6

(bets are high, frequent raises, many players fold)

Player:	A	B	C	D	E	F	G	Pot size
Round 1				*bet $5	raise $5	fold	call	
	raise $5	fold	call	call	call		call	$75
Round 2				*bet $5	call		call	
	raise $5		call	call	call		call	$125
Round 3			*bet $5	raise $5	raise $5		fold	
	raise $5		call	call	call			$205
Round 4			*bet $5	fold	raise $5			
	fold		raise $5		raise $5			
			call					$245
Round 5			*bet $5		raise $5			
			raise $5		raise $5			
			call					$285

Game 7

(bets are high, infrequent raises, few players fold)

Player:	A	B	C	D	E	F	G	Pot size
Round 1				*bet $5	call	call	call	
	call	call	call					$35
Round 2				*bet $5	call	call	call	
	raise $5	call	call	call	call	call	call	$105
Round 3			*bet $5	call	raise $5	call	call	
	call	fold	call	call				$165
Round 4			*bet $5	call	raise $5	fold	call	
	call		call	call				$215
Round 5			*bet $5	fold	raise $5		call	
	call		raise $5		call		fold	
	call							$270

Game 8

(bets are high, frequent raises, few players fold)

Player:	A	B	C	D	E	F	G	Pot size
Round 1				*bet $5	raise $5	call	call	
	raise $5	call	call	call	call	call	call	$105
Round 2				*bet $5	call	call	call	
	raise $5	call	call	call	call	call	call	$175
Round 3			*bet $5	raise $5	raise $5	call	call	
	raise $5	fold	call	call	call	call	call	$295
Round 4			*bet $5	call	raise $5	fold	call	
	call		raise $5	call	raise $5		call	
	call		call	call				$395
Round 5			*bet $5	fold	raise $5		call	
	call		raise $5		raise $5		fold	
	call		call					$465

From the above examples you can see that the slowest betting pace—minimum bets, few raises (five per game), and many players dropping out—develops the smallest pot, $58. Playing the same game with the same stakes at the highest betting pace—

maximum bets, many raises (twelve per game), and few players dropping out—produces the largest pot, $465.

Many interesting things happen between these two extremes. Game #2 with minimum bets, infrequent raises, but few players dropping did about the same as Game #3 with minimum bets, but frequent raises. In other words, if players tend to drop early and frequently, you can counteract this drain on the pot by raising more often. And conversely, if you know you can keep most of the players in by not raising, you won't affect the pot much either.

If you want to limit the number of players in a game in order to increase your chances of winning the pot (by eliminating some of the competition—players who might catch a better hand than you if they stay in), then frequent raising will be a useful means of keeping a good pot size and improving your chances at the same time. By looking at Games #6 and #7, you'll see that the same thing happens with maximum bets. You can keep the pot the same size with many raises and few players, or few raises and many players.

Games #4 and #5 also produced about the same pot size—$160 and $165, respectively. Yet the bets were low in Game #4 and high in Game #5. Even though there was a big difference in the *amount* of each bet, in Game #4 most players stayed in and there were many raises (twelve). While the bets were high in Game #5, many players dropped, and there were few raises (five). This illustrates very clearly how the *size* of the average bet in a game can be offset by raising and dropping patterns.

This brings us to another issue: whether to raise early or later in the game. Since there will be progressively fewer players as the game nears the last round of betting, by raising early in the game you'll build a bigger pot than by raising later in the game (if all other factors remain the same). Let's look at two hands to see how this factor can affect pot size:

Game 9

(eight raises are made, early in the game)

Player:	A	B	C	D	E	F	G	Pot size
Round 1	*bet $5	raise $5	fold	call	raise $5	call	call	
	call	call		call				$90
Round 2	*bet $5	call		call	raise $5	raise $5	fold	
	call	raise $5		call	call	call		
	call							$190
Round 3		*bet $5		call	raise $5	raise $5		
	raise $5	call		call	call	call		$290
Round 4		*bet $5		fold	call	call		
	call							$310
Round 5		*bet $5			call	fold		
	call							$325

Game 10

(eight raises are made, late in the game)

Player:	A	B	C	D	E	F	G	Pot size
Round 1	*bet $5	call	fold	call	call	call	call	$30
Round 2	*bet $5	call		call	call	call	fold	$55
Round 3		*bet $5		raise $5	call	raise $5		
	call	call		call	call			$130
Round 4		*bet $5		fold	raise $5	raise $5		
	raise $5	call			call	call		$210
Round 5		*bet $5			raise $5	fold		
	raise $5	raise $5			call			$270

Note the difference in pot size: $55. Yet in each game all bets were for $5 and there were eight raises. In round 1 player C dropped, in round 2 player G dropped, in round 4 player D dropped and in round 5 player F dropped. It cost players A, B, and E each $65 to play the game until the end. Yet in Game #9 they risked this $65 for a chance to win $325 and in Game #10 they risked the same $65 to win only $270.

If it cost players A, B, and E each $65 in both games, who put in the extra $55 in Game #9? The players who dropped, obviously. The point is this: when raising is done early in the game, it will cost the player who drops a lot more to play. But we've got to make another distinction: it won't cost more for the player who drops in the first round of betting before he puts any money in the pot; it will cost more for the players who drop out in the second, third, and subsequent rounds.

Who cares about the betting pace? A winner does. As illustrated above, you could win $58 or $465 in a single hand with the same number of players and the same stakes. Now obviously this difference is somewhat simplistic. At times you'll be the only one with a potential hand and everyone will naturally drop out. In other hands, four or five players may get hands they feel are winners. This kind of thing will affect the amount of money bet, the number of raises, and the frequency and timing of folds.

But outside of card differences, the betting pace is the thing that will decide how big the pot will be. If your group likes to bet the maximum, raise often and early, and stay in to see their cards, you're going to have a higher average pot size than another group doing the opposite.

Use the Betting Pace to Your Advantage

Once you've learned to recognize the betting pace, you can use it to make more money when you've got good hands and to lose less money when you've got garbage. For example, if your group tends to raise heavily early in the game, you should make a decision to drop or stay as early as possible. You don't want to be feeding the pot with mediocre hands.

Looking at it the other way around, when you're dealt a strong hand to start with, you'll want to see a lively betting pace early in the game in order to win the maximum pot. To do this, you've got to encourage the betting, by betting and raising yourself. One thing I noticed about Dave was that he was often the winner of very large pots. And most of the time he started out in those hands with top cards and completed his perfect hand early. A lot of times these were hi-low games and he went for half the pot, playing the contenders for the other half against each other.

Once in a while you'll be dealt a great hand in five-card draw, or a beautiful three cards in stud, and find out that, when you bet the maximum, everybody drops. This kind of thing discourages a lot of players from betting strong when they've got good hands. They think if they check or place a small bet they'll keep everybody in. It doesn't work that way.

How to Influence the Betting Pace

Whenever Steve and Mike are playing, I know the betting pace is going to be heavier than if they were out. Steve will nearly always bet the maximum on the first round if he's the opener. If he's not the opener, he's likely to raise the maximum. As the game progresses, his betting settles into a more average pace. Mike, on the other hand, doesn't like to play poker for small pots. If other people are betting, he may keep still, but if everyone checks around, he'll bet something unless he's got a totally bad hand. These two players keep the average betting pace up throughout the evening. Dave, on the other hand, only puts the pressure on when he figures his chances of winning are practically one hundred percent.

You can control the betting pace to some degree by choosing the amount of your bet and whether or not to raise. If you're in front of a player like Steve, you can place a bet with a good chance that he'll raise. If you're trying to step up the pace, make maximum bets, raise when possible, and use sandbagging if it's allowed. If you're trying to slow down the pace, your actions will depend on your position from the opener. If you're the opener, a strong bet by you may keep the rest of the group from raising. If there are two or three checks to you, a small bet may be best. Actually, you have to try out various strategies and see how they work with your group. No one method will have the same effect on all players.

Types of Games Played

The types of games played will affect the amount of money in the average pot during an evening. Basically, the more betting rounds in a game, the greater potential there is for a big pot. In straight five-card draw, for example, you have only two betting rounds, one when the cards are dealt, and one after the draw. By playing it high and low, you can add a third round by having a bet after the declaration. If you add a rollover to five-card draw hi-low, you increase the betting rounds to seven.

While some players dislike hi-low because they feel it's not worth winning half a pot, this thinking doesn't make sense. The pots in hi-low poker are going to be larger because not only will players going for high stay in, but also those going for low. In addition, there is more likelihood of back and forth raising.

Don't expect a new game to work with a group, however, if they're antagonistic to it. No matter how many betting rounds it has, if the players don't like it, they'll simply drop out early and not bet. Different groups have their own prejudices. Some, for example, hate wild cards. If you try to introduce them to such a group they'll simply drop out early and you will have gained nothing.

Some groups dislike complicated games. If they have to remember a lot of rules, they feel they're at a disadvantage. Or they're simply too lazy to be bothered. You may eventually get a group to like a game they initially hated, but it will take time. Introduce new games gradually, and do it on nights when you feel a favorable atmosphere. For example, if there's a particular player who hates new games, try to introduce them on nights when he isn't there. Then, when other players start to call your game, you won't be blamed as the instigator.

When a new player comes into your group, encourage him to play games he's learned elsewhere. Then if it's a game you feel you can use to your advantage, make a point about what a great game it is and how it's nice to have some variety for a change. If it's a game you feel isn't going to help you, agree with the hardheads in your group who don't like "those crazy new games."

Chips or Money?

There's something different about putting a chip in a pot and putting a dollar bill into a pot. At least for some people. If you're playing with cash now, a switch over to chips may help liven up the betting pace. One night, simply show up with a nice new box of good quality chips. Explain that the chips will eliminate the problems of making change and take up less space on the table. It will be harder for them to refuse if you've already bought the chips as a gift to the group than if you ask them for their decision ahead of time.

Accepting checks for losses is another way to loosen up the cash flow. If a guy comes with twenty dollars and loses it, he'll have to quit. But if he knows he can write a check at the end of the game, he's likely to stay to try to win back his losses. Check writing is also a way to avoid carrying large sums of money to the game.

Efficiency

The more time that's spent doing other things than playing poker during the evening, the less money you'll have an opportunity to win. If the game is held up because cards are not shuffled, someone's making a telephone call, or players are eating, the fewer games will be played. You can encourage efficiency of time use by shuffling a spare deck ahead of time, or proposing a system for shuffling and reminding the person whose turn it is to shuffle.

You can suggest that players stay out of a hand if they have business to attend to, such as telephone calls, or going to get themselves a sandwich. When the game is at your place, provide adequate space such as end tables for players to place their drinks, food, or ashtrays. Have sandwiches already made up ahead of time. Prepare the coffee during hands when you're out. By being such a host at your place, you'll encourage others to do the same.

By taking on a few extra tasks yourself, you can assure greater efficiency. There may even be other players who share your wish to play the maximum number of games and will help you. Get to the game early and help set up the table, count out chips, and make coffee. Volunteer to pick up the food, drinks, cards, and so on, if this is necessary.

During the game you can keep things rolling by quietly saying to a player, "It's up to you, Jack." Or, "The bet's five dollars, Jim. Are you calling?" Keep track of the bet, the number of raises, whose turn it is to deal, and remind the other players when they forget.

Raising the Stakes

Depending on your group, each member's personal financial situation, and desire to gamble, you may or may not be able to get them to raise the stakes. However, you can begin with subtle suggestions such as doubling the bet on the last round of the evening, and special games with higher limits. But it may be that you'll simply want to get into another game with higher stakes. Don't expect, however, for all your skills with one group to transfer instantly to another. It'll take you a while to learn the new group's playing style, and to learn to read the individual players.

Whatever methods you use to control the betting pace in your group, remember that the higher the betting pace, the more money will be bet during an evening. This means the losers will lose more and the winners will win more. However, you've got to take into consideration the psychological effects of such a situation. A player who may not mind losing $25 a week may be quite shaken when he starts losing $100 a week. He may have considered the $25 as spent on "entertainment," and played an enjoyable, loose, carefree game. When he starts to lose a lot more, his play may tighten up considerably.

So observe carefully the changes in each individual player as the betting pace increases. Choose the optimum method that will net you the most money in the long run. It may be that you'll want to leave the Monday night game you play with your friends the way it is, but seek out another group in which to win your big money.

Building Pots

BUILDING THE POT IN ITSELF isn't enough. What you want to do is build the pot in games where you have a good chance to win. Increasing the tempo of the betting, as discussed in the last chapter, is one way to build pots. It's a good way generally to increase the size and number of bets throughout the evening. In this chapter, however, I'm going to cover some more specific points.

Keeping Players In

It was pointed out in the last chapter that one of the factors that increased the total size of the pot was the number of players in the game. The more players who stay in for the early raises, the greater the pot in the end. This is why it's important to get a player to stay in for even one more additional betting round.

However, by keeping one player in the game, you may cause others to drop. It's a very delicate situation, since the choice one player makes about dropping or staying depends upon the actions of the other players. In some hands, if player A bets and B calls, C and D will drop. In other hands, they'll do just the opposite. Obviously a lot depends on the cards they hold, and if they're holding very good cards or very poor cards, it won't matter what player B does. But if they have a borderline hand, what B does will matter.

Timing your bets and raises is crucial. And of course, position is all-important here. In some cases, by not raising a bet, you'll be able to keep two or three players in who would have dropped if you'd raised. Sometimes you can catch a player by sandbagging. For example, look at the following betting pattern:

Player:	A	B	C	D	E	F	G
			*bet	call	call	fold	call
	raise	call	call	call	call		raise
	call	call	call	call	call		

Player G had a very good hand, and wanted to raise initially. But he felt that if he raised at that point, B and E, who had mediocre showings, might drop. Also, he suspected that A would raise because of his good showing and tendency to raise in such situations. B called after A's raise because he didn't expect C to raise back and figured the raise would be called around. Then when G did raise, B and E felt that since they had already paid for the first bet and raise, they might as well see the last raise.

There are cases where not betting will cause players to drop rather than stay. For example, if you check a good hand in the first round of betting because you're afraid to chase players out, and you want to wait and see what the other players do, you may lose out when everyone checks around. Now there's no pot to entice players to stay in on the next round of betting. So you'd better be pretty sure another player will bet before you check a good hand on the first round.

It's also vital to know why the other players are raising. Let's look at a sample betting pattern below:

Player:	A	B	C	D	E	F
				*bet	raise	fold

Let's assume you're player A. Now, why did player E raise? Suppose you're playing hi-low, and the hands are set up so that B and D look high, and E, F, and A look low. E may be raising, hoping to get F and A out so he can win the low half of the pot. If you raise at this point, and E has a weak low hand, he may drop out. If you call, on the other hand, he may think your hand is not that great and stay in. However, if he's a reactive player, he may figure that your call means you've got a good hand. In this case, raising may be the best bet because he may then think you're trying to chase him out. You have to take his double-think up a step to triple-think.

Getting Players to Drop

There are times when you'll want to get a player to drop in order to build a pot. Let's look at an example from a game of hi-low, seven-card stud:

Seven-Card Stud, Hi-Low
(bets are $1, $2, and $5 at any time, three raises maximum)

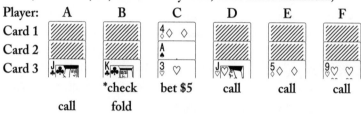

Player:	A	B	C	D	E	F
Card 1			4♦ ♦			
Card 2			A♠			
Card 3	J♣	K♣	3 ♡	J♡	5♦ ♦	9♡ ♡
		*check	bet $5	call	call	call
	call	fold				

In the first round of betting B checks. With three good cards to a low, and knowing that E is not an aggressive bettor, C bets $5. Everyone calls, except B, who drops.

Player:	A	B	C	D	E	F
Card 1			4♦ ♦			
Card 2			A♠			
Card 3	J♣	K♣	3 ♡	J♡	5♦ ♦	9♡ ♡
		*check	bet $5	call	call	call
	call	fold				
Card 4	8♣ ♣		Q♠	8♡ ♡	7♠ ♠	4♠ ♠
			*bet $5	call	call	call
	call					

In the second round of betting, C is high with the queen, and bets $5 again. Everyone calls around. C is disappointed that no one is raising, as he thinks he has a good chance to win the low

93

hand. He figures E is probably going low, but is too conservative to raise. F probably doesn't have much toward anything yet, and A and D are probably both going for high and worried about each other.

Player:	A	B	C	D	E	F
Card 1	▨	▨	4◇ ◇	▨	▨	▨
Card 2	▨	▨	A♠	▨	▨	▨
Card 3	J♣	K♣	3♡	J♡	5◇ ◇	9♡ ♡
		*check	bet $5	call	call	call
	call	fold				
Card 4	8♣ ♣		Q♠	8♡ ♡	7♠ ♠	4♠ ♠
			*bet $5	call	call	call
	call					
Card 5	Q♡		6♣ ♣	10♡ ♡	6♡ ♡	7◇ ◇
	*bet $5		raise $5	fold	call	fold
	raise $5		raise $5		call	
	call					

In the third round, A is the opener with a queen-jack high, and bets $5. Now C thinks if he can get D to drop, A will become a regular raiser. And since he now has four cards to a perfect low, with no 2s showing anywhere, he figures he has a good chance to get it, so he wants to build the pot. He therefore raises $5, hoping to knock D out, which he does. E, who now shows a 5–8–7 toward a low or straight, calls. F drops. C was correct in his prediction, because A now raises $5 and C raises back. He's not worried about chasing E out because he knows that E wouldn't be in this far without good cards and will probably stay until the end.

Player:	A	B	C	D	E	F
Card 1	(hidden)	(hidden)	4◇ ◇	(hidden)	(hidden)	(hidden)
Card 2	(hidden)	(hidden)	A♠	(hidden)	(hidden)	(hidden)
Card 3	J♣	K♣	3 ♡	J ♥	5◇ ◇	9♡ ♡
		*check	bet $5	call	call	call
	call	fold				
Card 4	8♣ ♣		Q♠	8♡ ♡	7♠ ♠	4♠ ♠
			*bet $5	call	call	call
	call					
Card 5	Q♡		6♣ ♣	10♡ ♡	6♡ ♡	7◇ ◇
	*bet $5		raise $5	fold	call	fold
	raise $5		raise $5		call	
	call					
Card 6	9♣ ♣		2 ♣		3 ◇	
	*bet $5		raise $5		call	
	raise $5		raise $5		call	

C gets his perfect low on the last up card. And E gets a 3, probably filling in his low. A, being sure of half the pot (if he's worried about E having a straight, he doesn't show any signs of it), bets $5. C raises. E calls. A and C take the last two raises and E calls.

On the round of betting after the high-low declaration, E also raises, indicating he must have gotten an even better low on the last card. But C figures no matter what E got, chances are it won't beat his perfect low. When the cards are turned up, E comes in second with a 6–5 low.

Player:	A	B	C	D	E	F
Card 1	Q♣	10♣	4♦	6♦	10♠	7♣
Card 2	3♣	6♠	A	4♣	2♥	5♣
Card 3	J♣	K♣	3♥	J♥	5♦	9♥
Card 4	8♣		Q♦	8♥	7♠	4♠
Card 5	Q♥		6♣	10♥	6♥	7♦
Card 6	9♣		2♣		3♦	
Card 7	7♥		9♦		A♦	
	HIGH		**LOW**		**LOW**	
	Winner		*Winner*			

The point of the above example was to illustrate how a pot can be built by pushing a player *out* of the game. A would certainly not be as likely to raise as much as he did if D was still in the game showing his strong heart flush possibility, especially if D got a heart on his fourth up card.

In hi-low games, having a strong or single contender for half the hand will increase the pot size because this player will raise every chance he gets. Of course you also need a strong contender on the other side to keep the raising going back and forth. You'll have to estimate carefully whether keeping players in, or chasing them out will develop a larger pot in the long run.

Build the Pot When You Expect to Win

The time to build the pot is on those hands when you think your chances to win are especially good. In order to predict these situations accurately, you've got to take two things into consideration: (1) your own hand, and (2) the other players' hands. Obviously, when you start with excellent cards, you know your chances are pretty good. If you're dealt four of a kind in five-card draw, for example, you don't have anything to worry about. But there are other situations in which your hand has an excellent chance of winning, based on the relative strength of your cards. In other words, you may have the best cards on the table.

Now we all know that poker is a percentage game. You won't win *every* hand that starts out looking good. You may be dealt three aces in the first three cards and end up with nothing better by the seventh card. You may be dealt a 6–5 low, but be beaten by a 6–4 low. The important thing is to recognize which hands are *potential* winners, and build the pot on each one. Even if you lose twenty percent, thirty percent, even forty percent of these games, you'll still come out a winner. So don't take it badly when you've done everything right, had the cards, and built up a beautiful pot, only to watch another player win it. This happens to all of us. You just watch for that next high-potential hand and build the pot up again. This one will probably be yours.

Recognizing a Big Loss

The trouble with a lot of players is that once they set their hearts on winning a pot, it's tough backing out. Let's say you start out with great cards, you read weak opponents around the table, and you start to build that pot. Maybe it's hi-low and you're raising on the low like mad with two players raising on high hands. You figure it's going to be the biggest pot of the night. And you're sitting pretty with a sure 6–5 low.

You're so eager on this one, you neglect that gnawing little voice that says, "How come Jerry's still in this late in the game? He doesn't show anything for high. What's he got?" Then you see Jerry get a low card and begin to bet. And you know Jerry never bluffs. His up cards show a 6–4–2. There are no 3s showing, and the only ace is in your hand. Now you know that Jerry probably has a 6–4 low. He's got you beat. And yet you can't give up that beautiful pot. So you ignore the truth and keep raising. You throw away $40 more in bets. Jerry wins the low half of the pot.

Once again we see how important it is to be a reactive player. The money you *save* by dropping out of the game when all the signs say you've lost, is money that you could take home as winnings. Don't be afraid to give up a pot that you've helped to build.

Modify your betting according to the chances of your winning. You may decide it's worthwhile to stay in, but simply to call or take the minimum raise in order to keep the bet low. But when you're sure you're beaten, and there's no way to chase the winner out, then get out yourself.

Check Yourself Out

In order to become an effective player, it's a good idea to check out your present behavior so you'll know how to modify it. The next time you play, observe yourself during games in which you start out with a good potential to win. When the pot gets big, how do you act? Do you accurately predict your chances throughout the game? Do you stay in until the bitter end no matter what? Do you miss the signs that another player's got you beaten? Do you predict accurately, but ignore the information and stay in anyway? Or do you get nervous and chicken out *too* often, missing out on pots?

Also, make a note of how much money it costs you to stay in until the end of a game after the point at which you realize your chances are no longer good for winning. In other words, let's say you're dealt four hearts in your first four cards in seven-card stud. The strongest hand you see around you is a potential straight. So you work at building the pot. Your fifth and sixth cards are not hearts, and you see your opponent's straight looking good and another player now shows three of a kind, with a potential full house or four of a kind. Everything you read about these players tells you that *they're* pretty sure they've got the winning hand. How much will it cost you to stay in the game from here on in?

The three of a kind bets $5. The straight raises $5. You call ($10 so far). The three of a kind raises $5. The straight calls. You call ($15 so far). On the last card you get your flush, but it does you no good. The three of a kind bets $5. The straight folds. You call ($20 total cost). The three of a kind turns out to be a full house and wins the pot. That $20 you threw into this pot is $20 less you'll be taking home at the end of the evening. In hi-low games, the betting is usually brisker and even more money will be thrown away. How much do you throw into the pot after ignoring clear signals that your hand is no longer in the running? Add it all up some evening and see what it comes to.

One thing I've always admired about Tom is his ability to fold when he thinks he's beaten, no matter what the size of the pot or what cards he holds. He could be sitting with a full house, but if he reads four of a kind, or even a higher full house in another hand, he won't hesitate to fold. Now of course part of the reason he can do this is that he's a good reader. But he's also got the self-control to avoid gambling. Even if he's wrong one out of ten times, that's not going to make him stay in those other nine. He's got confidence in his predictive skills, and the self-control to act on his predictions, no matter how tempting it might be to ignore them.

Manipulation Strategies for Pot Control

Various pressures, individual and group, can influence a player to change the amount of his bet. A free, loose atmosphere is created by such comments as, "Aw, it's only money," or, "You can't take it with you." Sometimes simply passing around sandwiches and beer will make the group feel more like they're "having a good time," and thereby part with their money more freely.

Very often a group that normally likes to bet and raise the maximum will make fun of a player who bets or raises the minimum. If the bets are a dollar, five, and twenty for example, a new player may bet a dollar. He'll be put down with, "A buck? Come on, make it five at least!" And conversely, a group who likes to bet conservatively may give a hard time to a new player who bets heavily.

In order to have maximum control over the pot without the other players being aware of it, try to have someone else do the raising for you whenever possible. For example, if you note a particular player doing well, you could make comments about how lucky he seems to be that night. Reinforce him when he makes a large bet or raise, with such comments as, "With your luck tonight, Jack, you might just as well raise every chance you get! Don't give us suckers a chance!"

If, on the other hand, you want to minimize the bet, you might try a sympathy pitch: "Hey, Jack, take it easy. It may be your lucky night, but the rest of us have to live too." Of course, you'll have to know the individual first. A comment that will cause one player to lower his bet may cause another to increase it.

Some players will be led by what they think is expected of them. If you say, for example, as you deal them an ace in five-card stud, "Big ace—ace has got to bet out," they may feel obliged to bet. Your comment has influenced their decision-making, and in order not to act flustered or stupid, they simply take your statement as truth and follow it. Another player might stubbornly refuse to bet simply because you made the statement. If you know your players well, you can control the situation either way.

Observe the players in your group to see what influences them. On some nights, does the playing seem to be looser, the betting heavier? What's different on those nights? What makes the group tighten up and play more conservatively? And what influences the individual players? You may notice a lot of manipulation going on already, conscious or otherwise, among the players. Take advantage of what's already happening, and try out your own strategies to control the size of the pot.

How to Read a Bluff

BEFORE WE CAN TALK ABOUT reading a bluff, we have to define what we mean by bluffing. For example, are either or both of the following situations illustrations of bluffing?

a) Jim shows four cards to a flush. He bets as if he had the flush, and if he does have it, it will be the winning hand. He doesn't have the flush, however, and knows it.

b) Larry shows a pair of 10s. He has another 10 in the hole and bets as if he has the winning hand. He thinks his three 10s will win, and bets on this basis. In fact, he is obviously beaten by a straight in another hand.

I think we can all agree that example (a) is a bluff. But what about example (b)? Larry's strong betting might scare out the player with the straight if that player thinks Larry's strong betting indicates a better hand, such as a full house. For purposes of our discussion, let's call example (a) an intended bluff and (b) an unintended bluff. Jim knew he didn't have the flush and was deliberately posing as if he did. Larry was betting only on his three of a kind and was simply unaware that his hand wasn't good enough to win. He wasn't intentionally bluffing, but the effects of his actions may have been the same on the player with the straight.

Don't Be Fooled by Unintentional Bluffers

Often it will be the inexperienced player who will pull a (b) type bluff. In his naiveté, he's unaware of what's happening around the table, and either under- or overestimates the worth of his own hand. You're likely to see this player drop out with a winning hand, as well as bet heavily on a weak hand. If he's unfamiliar with the various types of games played, he may expect the cards that won in one game to be a winning hand in another game where a much better hand is required.

Whenever a new player comes into your group, watch out for unintentional bluffing. Don't put too much weight on his betting actions until you've established his level of consistency. If you catch him in what looks like a bluff, ask him point blank after the hand, "You thought your straight was a winner, didn't you, Jerry?" Depending on the player, you may or may not get an honest answer.

Sometimes what looks like an unintentional bluff will merely be the case of one player not believing another player's bluff. For example, B stays in with his three of a kind because he doesn't believe C has his straight. B thinks C is bluffing. Clues to this situation are remarks such as, "You had it after all, you jerk."

The Intentional Bluff

When a player is intentionally bluffing, he will often bet and raise the maximum until the last round of betting. Once his betting and raising can no longer serve a useful purpose, such as getting the other players out, he's likely to drop out. Some players, however, realizing that their bluff hasn't worked, will then switch to hope that maybe the other guy was bluffing also and stay in for the last bet. This is usually a waste of money.

If a bluffing player stays in past this last point in the betting round, it's for one of the following reasons: 1) he was really an unintentional bluffer and didn't know he was beaten; 2) he irrationally hopes the other guy was bluffing too; 3) he wants to let the other players know he bluffs once in a while.

While some poker books recommend reason 3, it can be accomplished by other methods. A comment when you fold, such as "Nobody believes!" will work just as well. Or you could save your hand and show it at the end of the game, pointing out your attempted bluff. See the following chapter for more on this.

Reading the Intentional Bluff

There are some players who bluff very rarely and are particularly difficult to read. Dave is such a player. He's normally ultraconservative, but on occasion will bluff just to keep us on our toes. However, his bluffing is so rare and difficult to read that it doesn't pay to try and catch him. In other words, it makes more sense (and money) to *believe* him, even when he's bluffing. The few hands we lose by dropping out against his bluff hardly amount to much when you compare that with what it would cost to stay in against him on the hands when he's really got it.

Dave makes a big deal about the hands he bluffs, making sure we're all aware of what he's doing. Even if he's the last one in the hand, he shows us his cards so we'll know he was bluffing. This is to pique our interest, to get us to bite the bait. He'll often trap a new player in his net with an early, obvious, irritating bluff. He then has that player hooked into staying in against him the rest of the night.

What's the moral of this story? If you're not absolutely sure you're reading a bluff accurately, get out. That is, when you're playing against guys like Dave who bluff rarely. If you can accurately read the signs of a bluff, fine, stay in. But if you're not sure, it's better to lose that pot than end up paying a lot of money to see if you're right or not.

The Chronic Bluffer

The chronic bluffer is another story. If you believe him every time, you'd end up losing a lot of pots you should have won. He'd only step up his tempo and take further advantage of you. Mike was our chronic bluffer. Half the fun of playing for him is to put something over on somebody. He enjoys winning his bluffed hands more than the ones in which he really catches a winner. So it's the chronic bluffer that you want to decode as quickly as possible. Any telltale signs you come up with will be valuable clues and put the chronic bluffer in his place.

Early and Late Bluffers

Some players will try a bluff for an early round or two, and then quit if it's not effective. For example, if player D is trying to bluff out players B and C, he may try raising the maximum on one or two rounds. If he gets B and C out, he stays in. If he gets B *or* C out, he may try one more time. If he can't get either one out, he may drop.

Late bluffers will start their heavy betting and raising later on in the game. They expect their bluff to have more impact by waiting until all but the last two or three players have dropped. Then they lay it on heavy, as if they have no doubt of their winning at least half the pot. Sometimes late bluffing happens because a player doesn't realize until the end of the game that he's not going to catch his cards. Then he has the choice of dropping or bluffing. He chooses bluffing.

The bluffers who really build the big pots are the ones who start early and keep right on raising heavy until the bitter end. They're early starters who figure somehow that persistence will pay off. Unfortunately for them, the payoff usually has nothing to do with the effectiveness of their bluffing style. Any player they don't bluff out early is in because he's got possibilities. If the possibilities catch, nothing will get him out and the bluffer will lose. If the possibilities don't catch, the bluffer will win by default. If you can spot this bluffer and beat him, you've got yourself a nice pot.

The Second Reactive Level

In Chapter 4, I discussed active and reactive playing. The active player looks at his own hand and computes the odds of its winning in a particular game. The reactive player looks at the other players' hands and computes the odds of his having a better hand than those he reads around him. Bluffing, however, is done at the second reactive level. Player A reads the hands around him. He studies what is necessary to win in this particular hand. He looks at his own cards to see if they might *indicate* one of those winning hands. He puts himself in the other players' positions looking at his hand. Will they think he beats them? What will make them think he beats them? Through a combination of the cards he shows and his betting and playing style, he attempts to make them *think* he has that winning hand.

Therefore, to read a bluff, you should be able to retrace the bluffer's thoughts at this second reactive level. This means you have to be aware of what all the cards on the table indicate in possible hands. What would the bluffer have to have in order to beat all these hands? Do his cards indicate such a hand? If he's attempting to bluff with a hand that does *not* indicate a winner, there's a good chance he's either a) not bluffing, but sitting with a hidden good hand, or b) an unintentional bluffer.

Always Check the Cards First

Once you've thought out the bluffer's strategy carefully at the second reactive level, make sure the possible winning hand hasn't been eliminated by the cards. In other words, if the possible winning hand is a full house with 10s and queens, with three queens and a 10 showing in the bluffer's hand, how many queens and 10s are available for him to get? If you've seen all the other 10s and queens in other hands (folded cards, etc.), then you *know* he doesn't have that full house. He also couldn't have four queens. If you can eliminate all possibilities this way, then you have sure proof of a bluff. While a good player would never bluff with this information available, many players do *not* keep track of all the cards and might have missed this piece of data. So your first step in reading the bluff is to check the cards carefully. If you eliminate one possibility, make sure you've considered all others.

If there are cards available that might fill in the bluffer's hand, you can at least calculate the possibility of his having them. But of course, either he does or he doesn't. To say there's a one in fifty chance doesn't mean he can't make that one in fifty.

Body Language

Thanks to Julius Fast, Dr. Edward H. Hess, Dr. Alexander Lowen, and others in the field, most of us are aware today that our bodies have their own silent, but effective language. In his book, *Body Language*, Julius Fast tells us how the pupils of our eyes tend to widen unconsciously when we see something pleasant. There have been studies done of groups of people watching commercials to see at what point in the commercial their pupils widen. Supposedly, the widened pupils would indicate the best, or most attractive parts of the commercials. It would be interesting to observe carefully a group of poker players to see at what points during the game their pupils widened. If you could sensitize yourself to these changes, it would be easy to tell when a player picked up a good card. Obviously, the bluffer's pupils would remain small since he wouldn't be looking at a good hand. Unless, of course, he were aware of pupil dilation and able to fake it.

Facial Movements

But even if you can't see the other player's pupils well enough to use the above information, there are many other facial movements that might give a bluff away. First you should observe each player when he actually does have a good hand. Take note of such habits as increased blinking, wrinkling of the forehead, eyebrow lifting, smiling, frowning, lip sucking, teeth grating, twitches, and so on. Does he smoke or eat more or less when he has a good hand? Does he talk or laugh? Does he stare at his cards or do his eyes wander to the pot?

Once you've studied what a player's normal facial movements are during good and bad hands, match these movements up with his actions during a hand you suspect him of bluffing. While he may be able to control his obvious facial movements, and use these to *pretend* he has a good hand, if you can discover the subtle movements he's unconsciously making, you'll be able to read him.

Body Movements

What's the potential bluffer's normal posture when he has a winning hand? When he has a losing hand? Does he "guard" his cards with his arms when they're valuable? Does he sit hunched over the table, or lean back away from it? At what times does he lean back in his chair, tipping it off the floor? Or sit sideways with his legs stretched out? Get to know his normal body movements so that you'll be able to read them during a bluff.

Take Paul who always hunches over his cards when they show potential. Normally, when he has such a hand, he places his arms on the table as if to guard his precious hand. If he doesn't get one he normally leans back and begins to drink or smoke, leaving his hand on the table unprotected. After careful observation, I noted that, when Paul was bluffing, he leaned back and left his cards unprotected on the table, but did *not* drink or smoke until the hand was over.

The Poker Face

The poker-faced player attempts to eliminate body language clues by stifling such communication. He tries to prevent any facial expression and to use his body in a perfectly controlled, unchanging manner. By being totally unexpressive, he feels he won't give away any information unconsciously. The trouble is, unless you have a chance to play back a videotape of the game, most of us are unaware of many of the unconscious moves we make. We may control the obvious signs, but there will be subtle, telltale signs that we won't even be aware of.

The poker face in your group may be tough to pin down, but careful study should reveal subtle clues that give away his hand. Actually, it's not the poker face, but the deliberately deceiving player that presents the hardest nut to crack. See the next chapter for information on how to be such a player.

Handling the Chips or Money

Every player has a certain style of handling the chips or money. Does a player's style change from poor hands, to good hands, to hands in which he's bluffing? Does he throw out the money too quickly because he really has a good hand or because he wants you to think he does? Does he use a lower-valued chip or change when betting on a poor hand, as opposed to high-valued chips or bills when betting on a sure hand, or when bluffing a hand?

Some players will play light until the end of a hand only if they expect to win it. If they're not sure, they'll buy chips during the hand. To other players, it won't make any difference. Some players will be very picky about other players playing light or not betting in proper order only on hands that they think they're going to win.

Tone of Voice

A player's tone of voice can tell a lot—how tired he is, how hopeful he is, how sure he is, how interested he is, or how nervous he is. When you notice a change from a dull monotone to a higher register, with more rapid breathing and faster talking, you can bet some player has got a hand that interests him very much.

It's interesting how some players will only be concerned with their giveaway tone of voice and body language when they're bluffing. Normally, they don't notice their own behavior. But when they plan a bluff, they try to pick the most confident sounding tone of voice and posture to put up a front. What they don't realize is that this fake bravado may in no way resemble their tone of voice and body language when they *do* have good cards. This kind of player, in fact, will often play down his cards when they're good by acting as if he's got a rotten hand. So, by play-acting so hard, he actually gives clear signals to the careful observer.

Mood Changes

Very often a change of mood will precede a player's bluff. He may walk into the game one night in exceptionally high spirits related to others factors in his life. This euphoric mood makes him feel that everything he does is going to turn out all right. Even if he doesn't get good cards, he'll bluff as if he did get them. His high spirits help him put over the bluff because the other players attribute his attitude to the cards. They think he's reacting to a lucky night, whereas he's actually continuing in the same mood that he walked in with. If he's successful in his bluffs, he'll keep his good mood. But if you scent him out and give him a hard time, his good mood may fade as his stake dwindles.

Sometimes a player will have a mood change during the game. Art often does this. He may play a concentrated, careful game for an hour or two. Then when he notices that he's not winning, he gets disgusted with this method, grabs a beer, and loosens up his play. This is the time I know he's ready to pull a big bluff.

Players will change out of bluffing moods the same way. If they've had a string of unsuccessful bluffs, they're likely to feel chastised and refrain from bluffing the rest of the evening. Mike is the only player in our group who can fail at a bluff attempt three times in a row and then pull it again on the next hand. He figures by that time no one will think he's bluffing again. And he often pulls it off.

Nervousness

The change in level of nervousness may provide a useful clue in the detection of a bluff. Some players, like George, get nervous when they catch a really great hand. He just can't control himself when he's sitting there with a perfect low or a hidden four of a kind. He'll knock over his chips or stutter, or something similar. When he's bluffing, however, he's calm and controlled.

Joey, on the other hand, is just the opposite. He can hide that special hand without blinking an eye. But when he's bluffing, his level of nervousness goes up and he shows it in small but readable ways. His alertness goes up one hundred percent too, although he tries to fake a disinterested nonchalance.

Change in the Betting Pattern

A big bluffing clue is a change in a player's betting pattern. For example, a player may normally bet in a controlled, rational manner. When he has a good hand, he bets in order to build the maximum pot. In other words, he takes into consideration the fact that a raise or large bet at a particular moment might drop other players out of the game. He's also aware that his good hand may *not* be the winning hand, and carefully modifies his betting according to the possibilities he sees in the hands around him. Now, this same player when betting on a bluff may use an entirely different technique. He may simply bet the maximum and raise at every opportunity, which is quite a different betting pattern for him.

The bluffer normally uses an obvious betting pattern in order to let everybody know he's got a good hand. This kind of change in the betting pattern is an obvious clue. A more sophisticated player, however, will operate at the next level. He may simply stay in the game without making a lot of betting noise. He's counting on your ability to see this and take it to mean that he really has the cards.

In the final analysis, you have to first know at what level a player is working in order to read him. Active and simple reactive players will be more obvious and the signs easier to read. But players who are operating at second and third reactive levels may take a bit more decoding. You may not be able to read their camouflage at all in certain areas, such as betting patterns, but instead, have to find some subtle clues that they're unaware they're sending. Look for unconsciously sent body and facial messages or behavior changes. The time you spend in observation will pay off in the long run. But *never* tip a player off that you can read him. Unless you're doing it to psychologically hassle him, which we'll talk more about later on.

Bluff Your Cards

MANY POKER BOOKS CLAIM that bluffing should be used minimally, to keep the other players on their toes. In other words, if you never bluffed, it would be obvious every time you bet heavily that you had a good hand. By occasionally betting heavily when you don't have a good hand, you keep the other players from being able to predict your moves.

While the above makes sense, I think we have to go further and state that the good poker player is *always* bluffing. If reading and predicting other players is crucial to effective play, it follows that being *unreadable* oneself is also necessary. You want to be able to know what the other players are doing while at the same time keeping them from knowing what you're doing.

So far in this book I've been talking mainly about ways to figure out, or read other players. In this chapter, I'm going to start talking about ways to cover up, dissimulate, or bluff your own cards and actions in poker. At the same time you're trying to read other players, they're trying to read you. If they're successful, they'll have the edge. So you've got to do everything you can to camouflage your play.

Hide Your Strategy

Keep your cards to yourself. If you fold during a hand and later another player asks you what you had, you don't have to tell him the truth. Actually, you don't have to tell him at all, but rather than appearing secretive or unfriendly, make up something, like "a measly pair of eights." If you're confronted with a comment such as, "You couldn't have had a pair of eights—there were two showing and I had one," you can say, "It must have been sixes or something then—whatever it was, it wasn't worth staying on." Occasionally, tell the truth.

When you're sitting out a hand, never ask to see another player's hand. This way you won't be obligated to show anyone your hand. Some players will invite you to look at their hands occasionally, especially when they have an outstandingly bad, good, or interesting holding. You can repay this courtesy by inviting them to see your cards on hands that don't matter, or that will mislead them.

Show to Advantage

Show your cards on particular instances in order to create a specific impression. For example, you may want to impress another player with the idea that you will stay in and gamble on a long shot. Let's say you're playing draw poker and are dealt 3♥, 3♦, 8♥, Q♥, and 6♠. You'd ordinarily drop with such a hand, but since the bet was low, you use this opportunity to impress the player on your right, who has dropped out. You show him your hand and draw to the heart flush.

When you're successful in making the other players believe you have a certain holding when you actually don't, you may want to show your cards at the end of the hand even if all the other players have dropped. This depends on what you want them to think. By not showing your cards, the other players won't know whether you were bluffing or not. By showing your cards, you make it clear that you've bluffed. By acting proud of the fact that you put one over on them, you may even encourage some players to stay in against you in the future on the basis that you may be bluffing again.

When you've lost because of misreading another player, and end up with the second or third best hand, show your cards. There's no harm in looking stupid, except to your ego. We'll get into this more in the next chapter when we discuss bluffing your style.

Be Unpredictable

This should be the guiding principle in everything you do. Once you're predictable, you're readable, and this is exactly what you want to avoid. So don't do *anything* consistently in the game except win money!

This means you must avoid using any card system consistently, or at least avoid *looking* as if you're using one consistently. For example, let's suppose you use this system in five-card stud: your first two cards must add up to at least 19 points (or be a pair) in order to call the bet (aces = 11, picture cards = 10, others = face value). If you *never* vary from this system, another astute player is going to eventually catch on. This means he'll know exactly what your hole card is each time. So never act as if you're using a system, if you do. At certain times go against the system rules, and make sure the other players are aware of what you're doing. And of course, if your reading of the other players shows that you're beaten in spite of the system, get out; and the other way around, if you perceive that you've got them beaten, even though your system may tell you to drop, stay in. As we said earlier in this book, a system may be useful as a general guide, but it's the reactive player, who can read what's happening around him and act accordingly, who's going to be the big winner.

Replacing cards in five-card draw is an area where a lot of players fall into ruts. If you *always* draw three cards to a pair and two cards to three of a kind, the other players will know when you have three of a kind. Make sure that you vary draw procedures on occasion, and be sure the other players are aware of it, in order to minimize their predictive success. If you're a player who only stays pat when you have a pat hand, the others will drop like flies when you do. But if on occasion you stay with a pair, or three of a kind, or garbage you'll keep them guessing.

One night we were playing five-card draw, hi-low, with a rollback. Tom drew two cards. Normally with a two-card draw, one would expect him to be going for high. But on the rollback he indicated a low hand. Steve and Larry stayed in against him for low, figuring the odds were that Tom couldn't have drawn a good low with a two-card draw. But Tom ended up winning half the pot with a 7–5 low. Then an argument ensued in which Dave told Tom he was crazy to draw two cards to a low. Tom said he did it all the time and that it made sense because there was less chance of pairing up by drawing two cards.

Now Tom was not right about the mathematical chances of drawing two as opposed to one card for a low. But the point is, he left the group with the idea that he would often be drawing two cards to a low. And on top of this, some of them may even have believed his theory (especially with the proof from the hand in which he drew a 7–5 low), and may start to draw two cards to a low themselves. By being inconsistent, and making a show of it, Tom was able to effectively smoke screen his actions.

Body Language

Just as I suggested you learn to read the other players' body language in the previous chapter, here I advise you to camouflage your own body language. Make sure that you're not giving away clues with a movement of your facial muscles, a rise of the eyebrows, or some other physical mannerism. To do this, first carefully observe yourself during a game. Do you take a particular pose when you're winning or losing? Do you smoke, eat, or talk more during particular times in the game?

If you find it difficult to become aware of your body language, you might try initiating distracting signals to keep the astute reactive players off your trail. For example, start some nervous activity such as tapping your fingers on the table, fondling your chips or money, or scratching your head. Then do it inconsistently. In other words, do it both during hands when you're bluffing a good hand but have nothing, and also when you do catch the winning cards. Players who notice your activity at all are likely at first to connect it with *one* type of play. For example, player D may think you do it every time you're bluffing. So the next time he sees you do it, he bets into your winning cards. Even if a player waits until he's researched your nervous habit more thoroughly, the most he'll get out of it is that you're inconsistent. So he'll have wasted this time and maybe give up on you.

114

The other advantage of this kind of ploy is that it will distract, disturb, and otherwise annoy some of the other players. They may even complain about your tapping the table or stacking your chips or swinging your foot. But you'll tell them you can't help it. Your bugging them will interfere with their thinking and possibly even give you a reactive clue. It could be that player E only gets annoyed at your nervous habit when he's in a tight position himself.

Handling Chips or Money

Do you use a larger value chip when you expect to lose a hand? Do you have your bet all ready in your hand, anxiously waiting to throw it in, when you're excited about your cards? Do you have to be reminded that it's your turn to bet when you're not certain about your hand? Do you play light *every* time you run out of chips during a hand, or only on hands where you're sure of winning?

If you can use the above signals to read other players, they will obviously be able to use them to read you. So you've got to do something about it. One possibility is to be consistent. *Always* use the largest value chip possible. *Always* bet on time. And so on. Or, you could try inconsistency. *Sometimes* throw in small change when you've got a mediocre hand. *Sometimes* throw in small change when you've got a sure winner. By being inconsistent, you'll draw attention to your actions, but mislead your observers.

Voice Level, Breathing, and Talking Pace

Do you start talking faster when you're excited about a hand? Does your voice level go up when you're anxious or eager? Do you drop to a dull monotone when your cards are boring? Once again, carefully observe your behavior and take action to either be consistent so that your actions tell nothing, or totally inconsistent. In this kind of thing it may be difficult to be consistent. After all, you naturally start breathing faster and getting excited when you're dealt three aces in five-card draw. But you can at least try to fake that excitement once in a while about a hand where you're dealt a pair of 10s.

Mood

Does the mood you're in on a particular night affect the way you play? Do you bet heavier and bluff more often on nights when you "feel good"? Do you play more conservatively and less optimistically after you've had a bad day? Do you loosen up after the first three beers and change your style of play?

It may be difficult at first to deliberately change what you'd normally do in a particular mood. But it's important to do so. The next time you're feeling high and in good spirits, don't do what you'd normally do. Do the opposite. If you'd normally play loose and bet heavily, play a tight game that night. The other players, expecting your usual habits, will be thrown off by the change.

Betting Patterns

In Chapter 4, I said that most players develop a fairly regular betting pattern. You can tell a lot by whether they drop, call, bet, or raise. Especially when you match the bet with their cards, their position, and the prior betting patterns, unless you do something about it. The basic strategy here is to be inconsistent. Don't *always* check two pair in draw poker. Or don't *always* bet the maximum. Vary your actions.

Actually, you can have one consistent mode of operation that you merely spice up once in a while. You can *look* like you have an irregular betting pattern, when actually *most* of the time you use pretty standard procedures. Or, you might choose to *look* regular, when actually you vary your play quite a bit. By showing your cards and talking up what you're doing, you can create an opposite impression of your actual betting style.

Opening

What does it take for you to normally open on a hand? In five-card stud, do you require an ace, the high hand on board, or 19 points? In seven-card stud, do you require two or three good cards to open? If you require a particular minimum holding to open, and do this regularly, the other players will come to expect you to have this holding when you open. You may wish them to think this in order to effectively bluff a hand when you don't have such cards. Or you may want to hide the fact that you do this by obviously opening with less than the minimum holding on occasion.

Suppose you normally require two cards under 7 for a low hand or a pair of kings or better for high hand to open in seven-card stud, hi-low. You want to use this system, but you don't want the other players to be aware of it. So you wait until a hand is dealt where you see no strong competition for your half of the hand, for instance: low. You're sitting with an 8, a 4, and a 10. Four players check to you. You open even though your hand doesn't fit your requirements. If players on either side of you fold during the game, make a point of showing them your hole cards to bring the message home. If you end up winning the hand, talk up how smart you were to open on the 8–4–10 holding.

If you prefer a strictly reactive style, making your decision based *solely* on estimated value of your hand, you'll automatically look like an inconsistent player because you'll be opening with a particular holding in one hand that you'll check or fold on another occasion. In this case, you may wish to emphasize particular plays in order to look *more* consistent than you actually are.

Raising

Observe your raising patterns. Do you tend to raise mostly to eliminate other players? Or do you do it to build the pot on hands you expect to win? Do you ever raise for no reason in particular? Are you an early raiser or a late raiser? Do you raise only when you're *sure*, or when you feel the cards are coming your way?

If the player you're trying to chase is aware that this is what you're trying to do by raising, he may not be chased. He'll drop anyway if he has a bad hand. But if he has a questionable hand, he *may* drop if he thinks you're betting on the basis of good cards. He may drop even if he's not sure why you're raising. In the same manner, if you're trying to build the pot, you don't want everyone to *know* that you're doing it.

So make your raising unpredictable. Sometimes raise early, sometimes late. Don't *always* raise to build the pot when you expect to win a hand. Occasionally call, or bet, or raise something other than the maximum. Sandbag (if allowed) not only when you're confident, but sometimes just for the hell of it.

The important thing about camouflaging your betting and raising is that you don't overdo the acting so that it hurts you. Generally, you *do* want to build the biggest pot possible when you've got a winning hand, so you don't want to sit back and check or call too often. Try to utilize the situation to your advantage. Let the other players do the betting, raising, and chasing for you when possible.

Bet Out and Raise on the Wrong Card

Normally, when a player is dealt a good card, it increases his betting pace. When he's dealt a card that doesn't fit his hand, he won't be as eager to raise or to bet. When you see a player bet more confidently each time he's dealt a low card, you can assume he's going for low. His betting pace changes with the cards, and you can use these changes to read him.

You can use this knowledge to bluff your own cards. Let's say you're dealt a 2 and 4 down, a jack up, in hi-low seven-card stud. By betting out or raising on the first card, you give the impression you may be going for high. If your next card is low, you might refrain from raising a round to continue this appearance. Suppose your jack is a club, the next cards is a 6♦, and the next card an A♣. Your heavy bet on the A♣ after refraining from raising on the 6♦ will indicate to the other players that you're going for a club flush, or the ace in some other way helps your high hand.

Eventually, of course, as more cards fall, it will be difficult to make a low hand look high, or vice versa, except in unusual cases. But this method can be used effectively early in the game. Also, you can use it to give the impression you're going for a different high hand than is expected—a straight rather than a flush, or a flush rather than a full house, and so on.

Timing Your Changes

You don't have to be constantly doing a high wire act to keep people guessing. You can play fairly consistently one night and the next, play in an entirely different manner. Or perhaps just for the first hour. Since you require time to observe, make predictions, and check other players, they'll require the same in order to read you. Just as they start to figure you for one type of player, you can switch roles for half an hour and completely botch them up.

Change your timing during the game, too. If you usually bet out early, planning your bluffs right from the start, building up big pots for your solid starting hands, try something different. Hold back during the beginning of the game and come on heavy at the end. If your betting pace and playing style tend to change from early to late evening, once again, make a switch. If you normally play looser early in the evening, start playing tighter initially on some nights and switch to a looser style later.

Bluff to Win

Depending on the reputation you've developed, you may have more or less success bluffing to win. If you've exposed many hands that indicated a bluff on your part, whether you won or not, the other players may expect you to bluff, and therefore tend to stay in against you if they have a fairly decent hand. You may deliberately set this up and want them to think this way in order to keep them in the hands when you're building a big pot for a solid winning holding. However, in this case, you won't be using the bluffing hands to win your big money.

If, however, you've created the opposite image—that you are a player who seldom bluffs, one *who has it when he bets it*, then you may successfully use bluffing to win money. As long as you are the last player in these games and are not required to show your cards, you can perpetuate the image that you're not a bluffer. If someone asks you at the end if you had the flush, full house, or whatever it was you pretended to have, tell them you had it. As the last contender drops out against you, say something like, "Saved yourself a lot of money with the fold, Sam. Sorry to see you go." Or, "How come everybody always knows when I've got the cards?"

In executing the above bluff, however, make sure your reading of the other players is accurate. Don't try to bluff a full house when someone's sitting with four of a kind. Also watch out for the new player who's inexperienced with your group. He may not be as sure as the others that you "never bluff." Or, he may be one of those players who can't stand to be beaten out of a fair hand, one who will pay anything to see your cards, figuring his hand just might be better.

Choose your opponents carefully. Sometimes you'll want to be against the group's regulars, who "know" your style and will react properly to your signals. If you've carefully developed an image in the group, you'll be able to use it with those players who are astute enough to have read it. Other times, however, you may want to pull a different kind of bluff on a new player, based on your analysis of his gullibility, or his reaction to the image you've developed in the short time he's been playing with you. Some things that will work with one player will have disastrous results if used on another.

Bluff Your Style

I'VE ASSUMED FROM THE BEGINNING of this book that you're out to win money at poker. You may also enjoy the sociability and the food, but your prime motive should be to win. If you get wrapped up in the conversation or the drinking, you'll be sidetracked and miss opportunities for winning money. If you get hooked on the gambling and risk elements of poker, you'll make moves that are counter to good poker strategy. And if you get generous, sympathetic, or in some other way concerned about the poker welfare of any of the other players, it will hurt your game. Remember, no one forced anyone to come and play. If a person loses money at poker, it's his or her own responsibility. If you worry about the other players' ability to put food on the table and clothe their kids, don't play.

While every serious poker group loves a sucker to bleed, don't let unwitting innocents into your game. It will only create bad feelings and possibly more trouble than you had bargained for. One night I was playing $1, $2, $5 limit poker at my place with some friends. Four of us were sitting around waiting for the fifth to show up. Meanwhile a neighbor's son showed up. He saw us at the table counting out chips and asked what we were doing. Someone asked him if he wanted to play. He asked if we played for real money. We said yes, but that we kept track of it on paper and everyone paid up at the end of the game.

The kid was about eighteen. He didn't know how to play poker, but he started out with beginner's luck. That was too bad because it gave him the idea he was going to win some easy money from us. Our fifth arrived and we continued to play. The tide turned for Bobby and he started to lose badly. Every so often he'd ask me how far in the hole he was. At nine o'clock he was $32 in the hole. He said, "Wow, I've got a lot to win back." His mood changed from friendly sociability to sullen determination. At ten thirty I told him he was $87 in the hole. "Oh, God," he said. I suggested he stop playing because the chances were he'd continue to lose more rather than win the $87 back.

Then he told us he didn't have any money on him. Well, I put out the $87 and about three months later the kid finally paid me back, but it was a bad experience for everyone involved. When you play with kids, keep it penny ante, or play with chips, period. Another way to avoid the above experience is to play with money on the table, or to pay a banker for the chips initially. A paper tally doesn't seem real to some people.

Hide Your True Motivation

While it's assumed that the object of playing poker is to try to win money, you don't really want the other players to know how serious you are about it. Always give the impression that, while you enjoy winning (it's only human), it's really the sociability, food, drink, and fun that's bringing you back every week.

Don't sit there with a long face drinking coffee all night long. Be someone the other players will enjoy having in the group. Even if you don't wish to drink a lot because it impairs your concentration, you can sit with a bottle or glass in front of you all evening. You can nurse one drink for hours while the others are guzzling.

Dave was an obnoxious player. He let us know that he took a nap before each game. He wouldn't eat or drink anything except coffee during the night so he could concentrate fully on the game. When we played at anybody else's house, the host or hostess usually provided nuts, potato chips, sandwiches, or something to nibble on. But at Dave's house you wouldn't find a bite to eat and the only thing he'd serve to drink was coffee. So it was bring your own or do without.

When Dave was out of a hand and not interested in watching it, he'd talk loudly to another folded player without regard for those who were still playing. But when someone else tried to make small talk while *he* was concentrating, he'd tell them to shut up. Then he rubbed it in whenever anyone did anything dumb. And when a new player came into the group, he browbeat and embarrassed them.

Dave made all the other players wish he'd lose. Except Steve. Steve worshiped Dave. The two of them would spend hours discussing what happened. When Steve did something bright, he'd look to Dave for approval. Yet what Steve didn't realize is that his great friend Dave took money from him every week, while Steve was unable to turn his losses into winnings even after months of tutoring.

On the other hand, no one even noticed that Tom was a winner at first. While Dave and Steve were yelling and fussing about this rule or that, Tom quietly drank his beer, taking no sides and compatibly agreeing with whatever the group decided. Tom played the slightly fuzzy drunk who was just amiably going along with whatever happened. When he won, it was attributed to dumb luck.

Hide Your Skill

Don't come off as a sharpie, putting other players on their guard. Never let them know that you're watching them, observing in minute detail every move they make. And of course, when you do discover a mannerism or other clue that gives away a player's hand, don't let him know you're on to him.

The trouble with Dave is that he just had to talk about what a great poker player he was. Due to some kind of inferiority complex, he used his poker skills as a way to prove to everybody he was really smart. Now if he had really been smart, he would have shut up.

If you see somebody make a stupid play, don't mention it. When other players lose, attribute it to bad luck. Point out that they played the hand right, but luck just wasn't with them. Build up the egos of the other players, especially the losers, so they'll want to come back.

Show Up Your Own Stupidity

When you do make a dumb move in the game, loudly lament about it after the hand is over. "Oh jeez, why did I do that? That sure was dumb!" Sometimes you can make smart moves look like dumb moves. For example, if you fold a pair of 3s and later the winner has three of a kind, you can say something like—"What? Is that all you had? My straight would have beaten that! I thought you had a flush! Boy, was I taken in!"

The idea is to make it appear that when you win, you do so through luck, not skill. At the end of a good evening you can make a comment such as, "Boy, when the cards come like I got them tonight, a guy could win blindfolded!"

If you have players in your group who like to give advice, ask them their opinion and listen carefully to what they say. "Gee, buddy, what do you think I should have done with that hand? I wasn't sure what the best play was." When they point out mistakes in your play, agree with them. "Yeah, you're right. That was pretty stupid."

Another tack to try is to act like a gambler who doesn't care about the "right" way to play. You follow your hunches, and no one can tell you differently. When someone says, "What'd you stay in for?" You can reply, "I had a hunch, that's all." Or, "How did you know Harry was bluffing?" "I didn't. I just felt lucky." To complete this image, you can add some fine touches such as bringing a rabbit's foot to the game, getting up and walking around your chair in the middle of a losing streak, rubbing your hands and complaining to God when you're losing, or some other good luck fetish you concoct.

If you can hold your liquor, you might try Tom's stunt—looking like you're soused when actually you're quite alert. Even if you don't *really* drink a lot, you can make it look as if you had. Belching, hiccups, and slurred speech help make this image convincing. In the middle of your deal you can stop and fumble, "Oh yeah. Now, where was I? Am *I* dealing? What game are we playing?" You'll make the sharpies in your group think they can put anything over on you. Also, you can aggravate them and interfere with their concentration by not betting in turn or misdealing. But be careful that you don't get kicked out of the game for being too disruptive. What you want to be is a likable drunk, not an obnoxious one.

Getting and Giving Advice

A lot of advice was given around our poker table. There were many postmortems of hands, with varying opinions as to what the best way to play them might have been. At first I used to take all this advice seriously. Until I started to notice the discrepancies. Then I realized that not all the advice given was meant to help. Much of it was meant to confound.

Don't be misled by advice given around the table. Listen attentively and thank the giver, but generally ignore it. You can say, "I'll try that next time," or, "Next time I won't make that mistake." But don't let yourself be pressured by anything the other players say you should or shouldn't do. Make your decision independently. If it happens to coincide with someone else's opinion, you can say something like, "Yeah, you're right, Jack, I think I do have to replace the 10♦. It's my only chance." When you don't follow their advice, you can say, "You're probably right, Jack, and I know I'll be sorry, but I'm going to try replacing the 3♥ and see what happens."

You can be pressured by other's opinions either way. You may be so anxious to please them to show that you're doing the right thing that you listen to them. Or, you may be so annoyed that they had the nerve to tell you what to do that you do the opposite. In either case, it's dangerous to let their remarks have an effect on you. Don't get emotionally involved in the situation. Make your decision independently of anyone else's statements.

As far as giving advice, this depends on the image you want to create. In general, I'd say abstain from it. If you give bad advice, and the other person discovers it's bad advice, he'll have ill feelings toward you. If you give good advice, you're helping another player develop skills that will work against you in the long run. So keep your advice-giving to a minimum, without appearing to be the great stone face. You can get involved in a general discussion once in a while, and state your opinions, but do it in an offhand way, and never discuss anything really important. There are plenty of basic poker facts already known to most players, which you can enlarge upon if called upon to give an opinion.

Win Without Disfavor

It's not true that a group of poker players will always dislike a winner and love a loser. It really depends on how the player handles his winnings and losses. If a loser is constantly whining and complaining, making the other players feel guilty for taking his money, they may be glad to see him leave the group. Sometimes a loser will simply embarrass everybody. When a new player comes in, makes grossly poor judgments, throwing his money away, it can be a very embarrassing situation. Especially for the friend who brought him into the game. Sometimes, of course, such a new player will gradually catch on, improve his play, and become an acceptable member of the group.

We had a particularly embarrassing situation occur one night. Joey invited a friend of his, a woman, to play in the game. As they do with most new players, our group didn't give her a moment to assimilate herself. They immediately exploited her inexperience, played one complicated game after the other and further enhanced her nervousness by yelling at her when she didn't bet, show her cards, or fold in turn, according to our rules. After about an hour of this, an extra player arrived and we now had eight people. We agreed that with each hand, a different person would stay out. This was acceptable to everyone except Steve, who started complaining loudly that he couldn't continue playing in his present seat because he was being discriminated against.

"What's wrong with your seat?" someone asked him. He was sitting to the right of the new player, and when it was her turn to deal, it would be his turn to be out that round. He felt this unjustly discriminated against him because she was such a lousy player. Anyway, before we could iron out the finer points of his position, the woman got up and said she had to leave early anyway, so she would just leave now. Some of us insisted that Steve should be the one to leave, not her, but she left anyway and never came back. Being a woman myself, I empathized with her. Playing poker with this group required a thick skin.

Some people thrive on challenge, and you may get a loser back week after week because of his determination to win eventually. Others figure that the longer their present losing streak lasts, the greater chance they'll have at a long winning streak later. Some are simply addicted to their night out away from the family, and won't quit it for anything.

Generally, a winner who acts superior, and gloats over his winnings, is one that will be disliked. If you rub it in the losers' noses, making them feel inferior, they'll naturally hate you. If you talk up all the things you're buying with your winnings, like that cruise to the Caribbean, you'll only make the other players try harder to beat you. Of course there will be exceptions, like Steve. Hero-worshipers like this may lick your boots.

Bluff Your Style
Okay.

You're playing serious poker. You're carefully observing, analyzing, predicting, and planning your moves for the maximum take. But don't let anybody else know this. Act the part of a casual player out for a good time. Let the group know how much *fun* the game is. Let them know what a *gambler* you are. Give the impression that you play for kicks, and your style is accidental, not studied.

By bluffing your style, you'll be able to bluff your cards more effectively. The person who wins at poker is the one who knows the most about the other players' thinking and divulges the least about his own. Doing this skillfully requires effort and practice, but the more you work at it, the greater your rewards will be.

Bibliography

How Not To Lose at Poker, J.L. Castle, Little Brown & Co., Boston, 1970.

Body Language, Julius Fast, Pocket Books, New York, 1970.

Parent Effectiveness Training, Dr. Thomas Gordon, New American Library, New York, 1970.

I'm OK—You're OK, Thomas A. Harris, M.D., Avon Books, New York, 1967.

Oswald Jacoby on Poker, Oswald Jacoby, Doubleday & Co., New York, 1940.

Winning Poker, Oswald Jacoby, Permabooks, New York, 1949.

The Complete Guide to Winning Poker, Albert Hodges Morehead, Simon & Schuster, New York, 1967.

Scarne On Cards, John Scarne, Crown Publishers, New York, 1965.

When I Say No, I Feel Guilty, Manual J. Smith, Ph.D., The Dial Press, New York, 1975.

Advanced Concepts of Poker, Frank R. Wallace, I & O Publishing Co., Wilmington, Del., 1970.

Man's Choice, Frank R. Wallace, I & O Publishing Co., Wilmington, Del., 1970.

The Education of a Poker Player, Herbert Osborn Yardley, Simon & Schuster, New York, 1957.